COLL

## HOW TO IDENTIFY

# BUTTERFLIES

HarperCollins*Publishers*
77–85 Fulham Palace Road
London W6 8JB

00 02 04 03 01 99

2 4 6 8 10 9 7 5 3 1

First published 1999

Dedicated to my wife Georgina and my daughter Alexandra

I would like to thank Mr Martin Gascoigne-Pees and Mr Graham Giles, whose help has been invaluable in the preparation of this book.

Richard Lewington has lived and worked in Oxfordshire as a biological illustrator for the past 25 years. Specializing mainly in entomological subjects, when he is not painting he spends much of his time in the countryside, observing and photographing the natural world. Of the many books he has illustrated, *The Butterflies of Britain and Ireland* by Jeremy Thomas and *Collins Field Guide to the Butterflies of Britain and Europe* by Tom Tolman, are probably the best known.

ISBN 0 00 220123 2

Designed by Liz Bourne

Colour reproduction by Colourscan Pte., Singapore
Printed and bound by Printing Express Ltd, Hong Kong

# COLLINS
## HOW TO IDENTIFY
# BUTTERFLIES

## RICHARD LEWINGTON

HarperCollins*Publishers*

# CONTENTS

# CONTENTS

# Butterflies and Moths – Lepidoptera

WITH THEIR BRIGHT COLOURS AND LOVE OF SUNNY, FLOWERY PLACES, butterflies belong to the most familiar and best loved of all the 29 known orders of insect, the Lepidoptera.

Lepidoptera means 'scale-wing' and refers to the mosaic of scales which make up the patterns on the wings, that appear as dust when rubbed with a finger. These scales are varied in their structure and range from being hair-like, found mainly around the body and legs, to ornately flattened and arranged, tile-like over the surface of the wings. Most scales have pigment and produce the beautiful patterns of familiar butterflies like the Peacock and Small Tortoiseshell. On others the colour is produced by reflective structures within the scales which interfere with each other, giving the iridescent blues, purples and greens, that seem to change with the angle of the light.

Butterflies share the order Lepidoptera with the moths and although no single distinguishing feature, or scientific distinction exists to separate them, far more attention has been paid to the butterflies, even though worldwide, they are out-numbered by moths by more than ten species to one. Europe and North Africa have more than 400 species of butterfly but in the area covered by this book a total of 190 species occur. All regularly occurring species have been included, giving the butterfly enthusiast the best possible chance to identify any species encountered north of a line drawn from the mouth of the River Loire, eastwards and including Germany and Fennoscandia.

Peacock ♂

Magnified scales on a butterfly's wing

Lesser Purple Emperor ♂

Emperor Moth ♂

# Butterfly or Moth?

THE SCIENTIFIC SPLITTING OF THE LEPIDOPTERA INTO BUTTERFLIES – Rhopalocera – and Moths – Heterocera – is an out-dated practice and was used purely for convenience. However, the question, 'What is the difference between a butterfly and a moth?' is still often asked, though the answer is less easily defined. There are however several factors which can be used when assessing which is which but some of these are not definitive indicators. Generally, with practice it soon becomes possible to tell at a glance which of the two groups one is observing, with only a few species of day-flying moth confusing the issue.

## Butterflies

Butterflies are associated with warm, sunny days, when they fly purposefully, visiting flowers, pursuing mates and sparring with intruders. Some species however, will fly when it is overcast and very occasionally, after a hot day, at dusk.

Butterflies always have a club at the tip of their antennae. In most it is distinct, perhaps slightly hooked, with others it thickens gradually.

At rest and when roosting, most butterflies hold their wings together over their backs, usually with the forewings partially hidden between the hindwings. The Dingy Skipper however is an exception, holding its wings moth-like over its back. When perching, some other Skippers hold their wings in a characteristic posture, with the forewings raised at an angle and the hindwings held flat.

**Silver-spotted Skipper** *Hesperia comma* (left)
Typical basking posture of the 'orange' Skippers, with fore and hindwings held at different planes.

**Dingy Skipper** *Erynnis tages* (right)
In moth-like pose, with forewings roofed over its back and obscuring the hindwings.

**Marsh Fritillary** *Euphydryas aurinia*
Butterflies often feed and bask with wings spread.

**White Admiral** *Limenitis camilla*
Perching on a leaf of honeysuckle.

**Butterfly Antennae** (from left to right) Red Admiral, Large Skipper, Swallowtail, White Admiral.

# Moths

Most moths are nocturnal or crepuscular but quite a few fly by day, or are often disturbed from vegetation in the day-time.

The day-flying Burnets have slightly swollen and curved antennae, otherwise the antennae of moths are quite different from butterflies and diverse in their structure. In males especially, they are often ornate and feathery, being used to detect molecules released by virgin females looking for a mate.

The majority of moths rest with their wings held roof-like over their backs, with the hindwings obscured. However moths are more diverse in their structure and lives than butterflies and some rest with wings spread flat, whilst others hold them together over the body, like butterflies.

With few exceptions, moths have a wing-linking mechanism on the underside, between the fore and hindwings. This structure, known as a frenulum, can also be used to tell the sex of moths.

**Copper Underwing** *Amphipyra pyramidea*
In typical resting position.

**Burnet Companion** *Euclidia glyphica*
A day-flying moth with similar resting attitude to the Dingy Skipper.

**Frenulum**
This structure, present on most moths, is absent from all European butterflies.

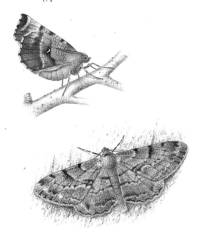

**Early Thorn** *Selenia dentaria* (top)
Resting in typical butterfly posture.
**Willow Beauty** *Peribatodes rhomboidaria* (below)
Resting with wings spread like a basking butterfly.

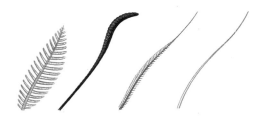

**Moth Antennae** (from left to right) Emperor moth, Burnet moth, Noctuid moth, Geometrid moth.

# Butterfly Structure

IN ORDER TO UNDERSTAND THE DESCRIPTIONS GIVEN TO VARIOUS PARTS OF A BUTTERFLY, it is necessary to become familiar with its structure, wing venation and wing areas.

At first some descriptions can sound confusing e.g. – the post-discal spot in space 4 on the underside of the hindwing – but once the features are learned, it is simple to identify the relevant regions being described. On some illustrations a line to indicate diagnostic features is included to assist in pin-pointing the precise area.

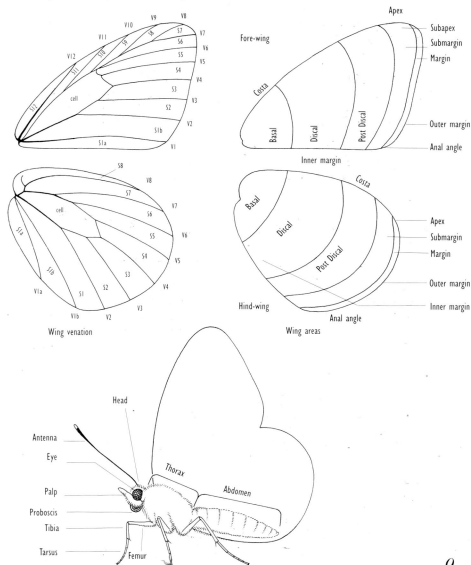

Wing venation

Wing areas

9

# The Butterfly Life-cycle: The Egg or Ovum

THE SPECTACULAR TRANSFORMATION, THE METAMORPHOSIS, FROM EGG TO ADULT INSECT, occurs in two forms known scientifically as Holometabolous and Hemimetabolous. Butterflies and moths, like beetles, flies and bees are Holometabolous and have distinct stages in their development, changing from egg, to caterpillar, chrysalis and finally, to the adult insect. Most insect orders are Hemimetabolous. These are more primitive and have no pupal stage, and include the dragonflies, bugs, grasshoppers and earwigs. Their stages of developmental growth are less distinct and their eggs produce nymphs or larvae that resemble the adults and grow by shedding their skin several times until mature.

Female Orange Tip laying an egg on garlic mustard

Eggs range from being large, smooth and spherical like the Swallowtails, to those of the Blues, which are tiny and have delicate, lace-like textures covering the whole surface. A central dimple called the micropyle allows sperm to enter and the developing caterpillar to breath; this is just visible with the naked eye in some species. The colour and appearance of eggs may change after having been laid, with some becoming brighter and more conspicuous and others, especially those like the Hairstreaks that over-winter, becoming camouflaged by algae and detritus. The female of the Sloe Hairstreak has another protective device for her eggs, which are covered with hairs from the tip of her abdomen. This is important for their survival, as huge numbers of insect eggs are predated by other invertebrates and larger predators, such as birds. Minute parasitic wasps account for the loss of most eggs and cater-pillars, the most familiar of these being *Apanteles glomeratus* whose yellow cocoons are often seen on walls and in sheds, surrounding the deflated corpses of Large White caterpillars (see p.13).

The eggs of all insects and the Lepidoptera in particular are incredible structures and for the butterfly enthusiast, a hand lens or better still a low powered microscope opens up a new world. Many eggs are easy to find in the wild, either by watching a female searching for a suitable egg laying site, or by learning the larval foodplants and knowing likely places the female may choose to lay. Most females are very particular about where they lay their eggs and take great care in selecting suitable plants, crawling over and fluttering around a likely site before carefully curving the abdomen and ovipositing. Some species however, appear less particular, for example, some members of the Brown family *Satyridae*, scrabble and flutter amongst vegetation and pump out their eggs apparently randomly.

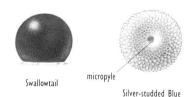

Swallowtail

micropyle

Silver-studded Blue

White Admiral

The three *Limenitis* species have distinctive eggs that resemble little spiny golf balls made from glass. These are laid singly on the upper surface of leaves but their close relatives, the Peacock and Small Tortoiseshell, lay their eggs in large batches, hidden on the underside of leaves. All the Whites

Some butterflies like the Marbled White and Ringlet release their eggs indiscriminately amongst grasses and are impossible to find. To obtain their eggs for breeding is simple, as the females release their eggs randomly when confined briefly in a muslin cage. Eggs usually hatch within one to three weeks of being laid but several species over-winter in the egg stage, often with the tiny caterpillar fully formed inside. With some species, notably the Hairstreaks, the discovery of eggs in the winter can be the best way of establishing the butterfly's presence.

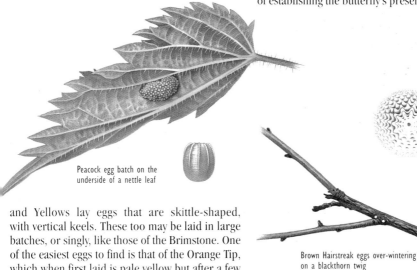

Peacock egg batch on the underside of a nettle leaf

Brown Hairstreak eggs over-wintering on a blackthorn twig

and Yellows lay eggs that are skittle-shaped, with vertical keels. These too may be laid in large batches, or singly, like those of the Brimstone. One of the easiest eggs to find is that of the Orange Tip, which when first laid is pale yellow but after a few days turns bright orange. It is laid singly, as the young caterpillars are cannibalistic.

For many caterpillars, their empty eggshell is the first meal they take and when breeding butterflies and moths, it is important that this first meal goes undisturbed, as it is vital for successful development.

Brimstone

Large White

# The Butterfly Life-cycle:
# The Caterpillar or Larva

THIS IS THE GROWING STAGE AND AFTER THE ADULT BUTTERFLY, the most familiar part of a butterfly's life-cycle.The newly hatched caterpillar, having survived as an egg, sets about its main task, to eat. Some begin feeding immediately, whist others, after eating their empty eggshell, prepare for hibernation without eating any vegetation. The Silver-washed Fritillary caterpillar is one of these. It remains concealed, in a crevice on a tree trunk for up to eight months, having eaten nothing since the empty shell. Once eating has begun, growth is rapid and apart from those that break for hibernation, some faster growing species can reach full size in less than three weeks. As it grows, the caterpillar's outer skin becomes tight and eventually splits to reveal a new, baggier skin in which to expand. Four or more of these moults occur throughout the caterpillar's life-time, each stage is known as an instar.

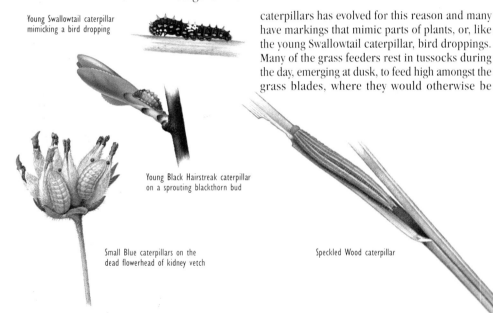

Young Swallowtail caterpillar mimicking a bird dropping

Young Black Hairstreak caterpillar on a sprouting blackthorn bud

Small Blue caterpillars on the dead flowerhead of kidney vetch

Speckled Wood caterpillar

caterpillars has evolved for this reason and many have markings that mimic parts of plants, or, like the young Swallowtail caterpillar, bird droppings. Many of the grass feeders rest in tussocks during the day, emerging at dusk, to feed high amongst the grass blades, where they would otherwise be

The shape and form of butterfly caterpillars is varied and although they cannot compete with the bizarre diversity of some moth caterpillars, nevertheless, many are attractive and some spectacular. As already stated the main objective of a caterpillar is to eat but of equal importance is to avoid being eaten. The appearance and behaviour of

vulnerable. Most of the Browns and Skippers feed here and it is not by accident they are green or buff coloured, with longitudinal white stripes. Fritillary caterpillars and some other members of the *Nymphalidae* family rely on fierce looking spines for their protection, some species living commu-nally. When threatened they move as one in sudden waves to deter predators. The Red Admiral and Painted Lady however are solitary and construct a tent made from the spiny leaves of nettle or thistle.

The caterpillars of several of the Blues produce a sugary secretion from a gland on the back. This is attractive to ants who eagerly seek out the caterpillars and defend them whilst protecting the sweet offering. The Large Blues however, have an ulterior motive in attracting ants, as their caterpillars feed on the ants' grubs, after they have been taken to the ants' nest.

The spiny High Brown Fritillary caterpillar, typical of the *Nymphalidae*

Brightly coloured and conspicuous caterpillars, like those of the Large White and Monarch, carry a warning that they are unpalatable and should not be eaten. They absorb noxious chemicals from the plants they eat and predators soon learn that these gaudy creatures are best left alone. The Large White caterpillar, which is one of the few pest species of butterfly, also has a repugnant smell that is well known to vegetable gardeners and growers of nasturtiums. Swallowtail caterpillars also give off an unpleasant smell, which is emitted when the osmeterium, a forked, orange organ, is inflated from behind the caterpillars head.

Large Blue caterpillar with ant grubs

Despite all these strategies that have developed to ensure the caterpillars' survival, the majority do not make it past the larval stage. Birds account for

Swallowtail caterpillar with osmeterium inflated to deter predators

many, though it is the caterpillars of moths, that make a major contribution to the success of many species of insectivorous bird. Other invertebrates are the caterpillars' main enemies, notably parasitic wasps and flies, which manage to counter the

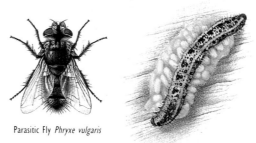

Parasitic Fly *Phryxe vulgaris*

The cocoons of the parasitic wasp *Apanteles glomeratus* surrounding the corpse of a Large White caterpillar

various protective devices set against them. They lay their eggs on or in the young larva and the grubs feed on the living caterpillar, leaving its main organs intact, thus retaining a constant supply of fresh food. Bacteria and viruses are also responsible for the death of many caterpillars, leaving them hanging lifeless from the vegetation.

# The Butterfly Life-cycle:
# The Chrysalis or Pupa

THE PUPAL STAGE IN THE BUTTERFLY'S LIFE-CYCLE IS THE PERIOD OF GREATEST VULNERABILITY and the lack of mobility of the chrysalis makes camouflage and concealment important factors in its survival. Three basic methods of pupation are employed, depending on the species but more than one of these methods may be found within a family.

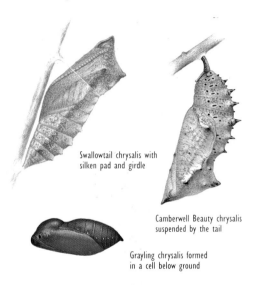

Swallowtail chrysalis with silken pad and girdle

Camberwell Beauty chrysalis suspended by the tail

Grayling chrysalis formed in a cell below ground

Admirals, Fritillaries and many of the Browns, suspend their chrysalises by their rear end, from a silken pad, attached to the foodplant or other support. Some, like the Red Admiral and Dark Green Fritillary, are concealed within a tent constructed from leaves of the foodplant, or in a loose cocoon in the vegetation but others are less well hidden and rely on their cryptic camouflage for their survival. The chrysalises of some of the

Orange Tip

Black Hairstreak

Meadow Brown chrysalis, formed low down in grassy tussocks

Swallowtails, the Whites and some of the Blues, attach themselves by their rear end, in an upright position, to a silken pad, supported around the middle, by a fine silken girdle. The colour of these chrysalises is variable, usually a shade of brown or green depending on the colour of the surrounding vegetation or the background. Most are formed without being hidden away, or enclosed in a cocoon but they are rarely found in the wild. The Orange tip is a good example. It spends ten months as a buff, or much more rarely a green, coloured chrysalis but other than captive bred specimens, few people have ever seen it. Those of the Small White however, are perhaps more familiar. Seen on walls and buildings, they are brown and well spotted but when they pupate on the foodplant, the ground colour is green and plainer.

Nymphalids are particularly beautiful, being adorned with silvery spots and metallic flushes, which are said to resemble droplets of dew, reflecting the sunlight on withered leaves. Two exceptions in this family are the Purple Emperor and Lesser Purple Emperor whose chrysalises are remarkable, perfectly matching the pale green underside of sallow and aspen leaves.

Invertebrates make the greatest impact on survival rates, with parasitic wasps, again causing the most damage. Timing is essential for some of these parasites, as many are tiny and can only pierce the chrysalis's body while it is still soft, immediately the larval skin has been shed. Some of the larger wasps however, have no trouble in piercing the hardened skin but are often deterred from injecting their eggs, by the vigorous wriggling employed by some chrysalises. The Painted Lady chrysalis can make nettles and thistles shake, in its desperate struggle to evade the needle-like ovipositor of the ichneumon wasp.

Two colour forms of Small White chrysalises

Those chrysalises that lack any silken support or attachment, are usually concealed under or close to the ground, either in an earth chamber like the Grayling, or deep in grassy tussocks like several other Brown butterflies. In these situations they are vulnerable to attack by ground predators, with small mammals and birds, taking their toll. Like their caterpillars, the chrysalises of some of the Blues and Hairstreaks live in the company of ants and may pupate in their brood chambers. Some have the remarkable ability of producing a rasping squeak which is thought to attract the ants and so give protection from potential predators.

The leaf-like Purple Emperor chrysalis

Chrysalises that do not survive may sometimes be found hanging still and lifeless, with only the exit holes of the newly hatched parasites to reveal the story.

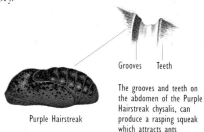

Silver-washed Fritillary

Small Tortoiseshell

Grooves    Teeth

Purple Hairstreak

The grooves and teeth on the abdomen of the Purple Hairstreak chysalis, can produce a rasping squeak which attracts ants

# Papilionidae – The Swallowtails and Apollos

EUROPE 11 species; NORTHERN EUROPE 4 species; BRITAIN 1 resident species

Mainly large, boldly marked butterflies, with a strong, gliding flight, and tails on the hindwings of the Swallowtails. Apollos have a more laborious flapping flight and lack tails. Sexes are similar, though the females are usually larger and Apollo females are more heavily dusted with black. During mating, Apollos produce a sphragis, a hard structure at the end of the female's abdomen, to prevent further copulation. Eggs are laid singly and are spherical or bun-shaped and may be smooth or granular. Caterpillars of some species have an osmeterium, a brightly coloured inflatable organ, behind the head, which helps protect them from attack by predators. Chrysalises may be cryptically coloured and attached by a silken pad and girdle, or, like the Apollos, secreted on the ground beneath moss.

Swallowtail ♂

Apollo ♂

# Pieridae – The Whites and Yellows

EUROPE 46 species; NORTHERN EUROPE 20 species;
BRITAIN 6 resident species, 1 common migrant

A large family of light, or brightly coloured, medium-sized butterflies, with females often more heavily marked with black. Some, like the Large White and Clouded Yellow, are strong, long distance migrants, whilst others, notably the Wood White, flutter feebly in localised colonies. Contains some of the few pest species, who lay their skittle-shaped eggs either singly or in large batches. Their caterpillars are mostly green and well camouflaged but some are conspicuous and gregarious, containing unpleasant chemicals to deter predators. Chrysalises have pointed or beak-shaped heads and are held by a silken pad and girdle. Their colour varies according to the background on which they are formed.

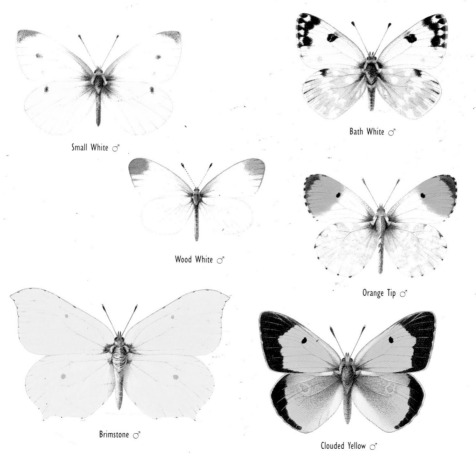

Small White ♂

Bath White ♂

Wood White ♂

Orange Tip ♂

Brimstone ♂

Clouded Yellow ♂

# Lycaenidae – The Hairsteaks, Coppers and Blues

## Europe 105 species; Northern Europe 49 species; Britain 16 Resident species

This large family includes some of the smallest butterflies, many of whom are also the most brilliantly coloured. The sexes are often dissimilar and several species that have metallic blue males, have females that are much duller and less conspicuous. Lycaenid eggs are laid singly and are intricately patterned, resembling tiny pieces of sculptured porcelain. Their caterpillars are inactive and woodlouse-shaped, with many living in close association with ants. Protection is gained from the ants, in return for a sugary meal, exuded from a gland on the back. Those of the five species of Large Blue have developed the relationship further and feed on the ant larvae after being taken into their nest. Chrysalises are plump and rounded, either attached by a pad of silk and a girdle, or hidden away below ground, without any silken support.

Purple Hairstreak ♂

Brown Hairstreak ♂

Black Hairstreak ♂

Green Hairstreak ♂

Small Copper ♂

Brown Argus ♂

Large Blue ♂

Large Copper ♂

Adonis Blue ♂

♀

# Riodinidae – Duke of Burgundy

EUROPE 1 species; NORTHERN EUROPE 1 species; BRITAIN 1 resident species

A single, unspectacular species, belonging to a large, diverse and mainly tropical family. The male has only two pairs of fully functional legs, whereas all three pairs are used by the female. She is also slightly larger and more brightly marked. The caterpillar is sluggish and resembles that of a bristly Lycaenid.

Duke of Burgundy ♂

# Danaidae – The Monarch

EUROPE 2 species; NORTHERN EUROPE 1 migrant species; BRITAIN 1 migrant species

Large, orange and black butterflies with white markings and a strong, flapping and gliding flight. The sexes are similar, though the male has a distinctive black sex-brand on vein 2 of the hindwings. They have two pairs of functional legs. Caterpillars ingest toxins from their foodplants, rendering the following stages unpalatable to most predators. The plump chrysalis is suspended, head downwards from a silken pad.

Monarch ♂

19

# Nymphalidae – The Admirals, Tortoiseshells and Fritillaries

**EUROPE 66 species; NORTHERN EUROPE 49 species; BRITAIN 14 resident species, 2 common migrants**

Some of the most spectacular and beautiful butterflies belong to this large and diverse family, which contains several well known migrants. All have two pairs of functional legs. Eggs are laid either singly or in large batches and are usually conical, with longitudinal keels. Some caterpillars live gregariously and many species are adorned with rows of protective spines. Chrysalises are often attractively marked with silvery, metallic spot and spines, and are suspended from a silken pad by their tail end.

Red Admiral ♂

Purple Emperor ♂

Small Tortoisehell ♂

Comma ♂

Pearl-bordered Fritillary ♂

Heath Fritillary ♂

# Satyridae – The Browns

EUROPE 120 species; NORTHERN EUROPE 46 species; BRITAIN 11 resident species

Mainly dark brown or ochreous butterflies with characteristic, white pupiled eye-spots, especially prominent at the tip of the forewings. There are however, exceptions, the main one being the Marbled White, which superficially resembles a member of the *Pieridae* family. Like all Satyrids though, it has only two pairs of functional legs. All species have caterpillars that feed on grasses or sedges, they are typically cryptically coloured, taper at both ends and have two tail-like projections. Their chrysalises are either suspended by their tail end, like those of the *Nymphalidae*, or are formed on or under the ground, amongst moss or stones.

Marbled White ♂

Scotch Argus ♂

Grayling ♂

Speckled Wood ♂

Meadow Brown ♂

Large Heath ♂

Wall ♂

# Hesperiidae – The Skippers

## Europe 40 species; Northern Europe 20 species; Britain 8 resident species

A family of fairly small, fast flying butterflies, thought by some to be more closely related to moths than to butterflies. They have stout bodies, with broad heads and large, widely separated eyes, adorned above with hair tufts. Males of some species have a sex-brand on the forewings, whilst others have a fold at the front edge of the wing, containing scent scales.

Grizzled Skipper ♂

Dingy Skipper ♂

Chequered Skipper ♂

Small Skipper ♂

Large Skipper ♂

TOTAL: Europe 391 species; Northern Europe 190 species; Britain 57 resident species, 3 common migrants, plus about 8 rare vagrants, including the Monarch.

# The Identification of Butterflies

FOR HUNDREDS OF YEARS MUCH OF OUR KNOWLEDGE ABOUT THE BEHAVIOUR and distribution of butterflies has come from the observations of amateur lepidopterists and naturalists, curious to learn more about the natural world. It is a continuing process and every year new information is being added, often about species that are common and already well documented.

Before any information can be noted and recorded, it is necessary to correctly identify the butterfly being observed and a number of factors may be taken into account, particularly if a detailed view is difficult to obtain. In northern Europe, many butterflies are fairly easily identified but a few groups and sub-families are confusing and can cause problems.

## THE JIZZ

The term 'jizz', recently introduced by Birders to identify a species from a number of general features including shape, size, movement and posture, has been adopted by dragonfly observers and is appropriate for the butterfly watcher. Observations, when just a fleeting glance or distant view is had, can be sufficient to identify some butterflies without the need for detailed views of wing markings etc. Sketching can be useful and it should be noted that a butterfly's appearance in the field may be quite different from its formal portrayal in a field guide, where illustrations are in the 'set' position, best showing the full extent of the wing markings. A pair of close focus binoculars can also be a great aid in observing butterflies that are just out of easy viewing range.

## HABITAT

Some species of butterfly can be found in diverse habitats ranging from city gardens to barren mountain slopes. Others however, are far more specific in their requirements and apart from the correct soil type and flora, may also need a particular sunny aspect or shelter from the wind. For this reason it is wise to note these features when recording, so that certain species can be discounted. For example, a bright blue butterfly flying around and basking on shrubs in a town garden is unlikely to be an Adonis Blue. It lives on south facing calcareous downland, with short, flower rich turf containing horseshoe vetch. It is therefore more likely a Holly Blue being observed.

## SEASON

The time of year a butterfly is seen can sometimes aid in its identification, particularly if it is a species that has a restricted flight period. Several of the Hairstreaks for example often fly high without settling for long but a Hairstreak silhouetted above a blackthorn hedge in August, couldn't be a Black Hairstreak, as it rarely flies later than mid-July. The Brown Hairstreak is therefore a more likely candidate. Nevertheless, flight periods for butterflies vary, depending on the locality, with more extended periods and a greater number of broods produced further south. The weather is also a factor and some seasons may be brought forward or delayed by up to two or three weeks in unseasonable years.

# Swallowtail

*Papilio machaon*

This large, spectacular butterfly is found throughout Europe but in Britain it is restricted to the fens of Norfolk where it is represented by the sub-species *britannicus*. It has a preference for purple and pink flowers such as ragged robin and red campion and as it feeds, its restless fluttering can make it difficult to photograph. Adults live for about three weeks.

Young caterpillar resembling a bird dropping x 1½

Swallowtail sub-species *britannicus* feeding at the flowers of ragged robin

Mature caterpillar x 1½

| | | |
|---|---|---|
| J | ▸ | |
| F | ▸ | |
| M | ▸ | |
| A | ▸ | |
| M | • ⁄ ▸ | ✘ |
| J | • ⁄ ▸ | ✘ |
| J | • ⁄ ▸ | ✘ |
| A | • ⁄ ▸ | ✘ |
| S | ▸ | ✘ |
| O | ▸ | |
| N | ▸ | |
| D | ▸ | |

**KEY FEATURES:** The striking yellow and black markings and the powerful flight are distinctive and its restricted occurrence in eastern Britain make it impossible to confuse with other butterflies. In the rest of Europe sub-species *gorganus* is less heavily marked with black.

**HABITAT:** The fens of the Norfolk Broads are its only permanent stronghold in Britain, as the introduced butterflies at Wicken Fen, Cambridgeshire have not been seen recently. *Gorganus* occasionally occurs in southern Britain and it is this butterfly that is the most familiar Swallowtail in the rest of Europe. Here, it is tolerant of drier and more varied habitats and occurs from coastal districts to over 2000m.

**FREQUENCY:** Widely distributed and common throughout much of Europe but declining in some areas due to loss of habitat. Local in Britain.

**LIFE HISTORY:** The eggs are laid singly on leaves of fennel, wild carrot, angelicas and rues but in England, milk parsley is the only foodplant used (see p.10) The caterpillar resembles a bird dropping when small but turns pale green banded with black, making it conspicuous to predators. However it has a fleshy forked organ called an osmeterium behind its head, which it inflates when alarmed. This emits an unpleasant smell to deter attackers (see p.13). The chrysalis, which may be brown or green, is formed amongst vegetation, where those of the second generation remain throughout the winter until the following May (see p.14).

The sexes are alike, though the female is often larger with a fatter abdomen. The continental sub-species *gorganus*, shown above, is more yellow than sub-species *britannicus*.

## LOOKALIKES

**Scarce Swallowtail** *Iphiclides podalirius*
Rarely seen further north than northern France, this is the only other Swallowtail to be found in the region. It has become less common in recent years but it is more often encountered than its name suggests, particularly in the south. Paler than the Swallowtail, some specimens being almost white, with wings transversed by tapering black bands. The tails on the hindwings are longer than any other European Swallowtail.

Appears from March to October in one or two generations. It lays its eggs on blackthorn and other *Prunus* species, and its green caterpillar, unlike the Swallowtail, is well camouflaged amongst the leaves. It pupates into a green or brown chrysalis and remains in this stage throughout the winter.

# Apollo
## *Parnassius apollo*

This grand butterfly, legally protected in several countries, is extremely variable and has many named sub-species and forms. Its size and heavy flight, interspersed with elegant glides, make it an impressive sight on flowery mountain slopes, though it has become less common in some areas. When threatened Apollos make a hissing sound and their forewings move up and down to expose and then obscure their red eyes. After mating the female carries a hard shiny structure at the end of the abdomen (sphragis), this is formed by the male to prevent further matings.

Female Apollo on white sedum, the larval foodplant

J ·
F ·
M · /
A · /
M · / ) 🦋
J · / ) 🦋
J · ) 🦋
A · 🦋
S · 🦋
O ·
N ·
D ·

**KEY FEATURES:** The large chalky white wings have varying amounts of grey dusting, some females being very heavily marked. The black blotches, with red centres on the hindwings, are unique amongst butterflies of the region.

**HABITAT:** In central and southern Europe it is found in flowery mountainous areas to over 2000m, but in Fennoscandia there are some areas in eastern Sweden and Gotland where it flies in the lowlands.

**FREQUENCY:** A local and declining butterfly particularly in northern Europe.

**LIFE HISTORY:** The large bun-shaped egg is laid singly on stems close to the caterpillar's foodplant, which is mainly white sedum or, more rarely, other sedum species. Here it overwinters with the fully formed caterpillar within, and hatches in early spring. The black velvety caterpillar has two rows of bright orange spots running down its back and is active only in warm sunshine. Like the Swallowtail, it possesses an osmeterium to deter predators. The chrysalis is formed in May, it has a white powdery bloom and is secreted within a loose silken cocoon beneath rocks or moss, where it remains for about three weeks.

♂

A variable butterfly, sub-species *apollo* shown here, is found in Sweden. It is one of the largest and whitest of the many forms.

♀

## LOOKALIKES

**Clouded Apollo** *Parnassius mnemosyne*
Smaller, with blacker veins than the Apollo and without red eye-spots on the hindwings. It appears from May to August in one generation, and in flight is heavy and greyish-white in appearance. In central Europe it is a mountain species but in Fennoscandia this rare butterfly occurs from coastal regions to damp open woodlands. The caterpillar is similar to but smaller than the Apollo and it feeds on various species of Corydalis.

♂

# Black-veined White

*Aporia crataegi*

Though generally common in continental Europe, the Black-veined White became extinct in Britain in the 1920s and remains so, despite several attempts at reintroduction. It is an active species with a strong, Apollo-like flight, which feeds avidly from a variety of wild flowers as well as communally from muddy patches. During mating the female grasps and rubs the male between her wings causing scale loss, which gives her a transparent appearance.

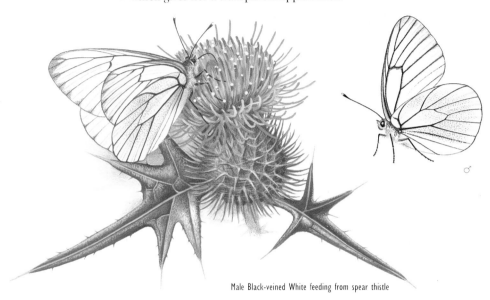

Male Black-veined White feeding from spear thistle

| | |
|---|---|
| J | / |
| F | / |
| M | / |
| A | / |
| M | / ♪ 🦋 |
| J | · / ♪ 🦋 |
| J | · / 🦋 |
| A | · / |
| S | / |
| O | / |
| N | / |
| D | / |

**KEY FEATURES:** Distinctive black veins on milk white wings, often ending in grey triangular marginal markings. The female has brown veins and her wings are more translucent and ochreous, especially along the costal margins of the forewings. The white tips of the female's antennae are bolder than those of the male.

**HABITAT:** Hedgerows and damp scrubby woodland. Orchards and meadows where flowers are abundant.

**FREQUENCY:** Quite common some years when the larvae may be a pest of fruit trees, however at other times it may be much less abundant.

**LIFE HISTORY:** Batches of up to 200 yellow eggs are laid on the leaves of blackthorn, hawthorn and cultivated varieties of plum, apple and pear. They hatch after about three weeks and after eating their eggshells the small caterpillars spin a silken web and live communally feeding in regimented groups until October. Despite the protection given by the web and the offensive smell of the larvae, many fall prey to *Apanteles* wasps similar to those that parasitise the commoner Whites. In the autumn they construct a dense web in which to hibernate. They emerge the following spring to continue their growth, and pupate in May, having spent eleven months in the larval stage. One generation is produced lasting into July.

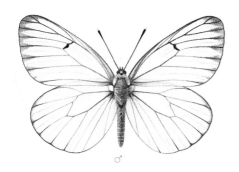

x 1½

The female is larger and duller than the male with paler marginal markings. Caterpillars live in groups until nearly fully grown.

# LOOKALIKES

**Large White** *Pieris brassicae*
About the same size but lacks the black veins. Both sexes have conspicuous black wing-tips and spots. (See p.30)

**Clouded Apollo**
*Parnassius mnemosyne*
Heavier and less active than the Black-veined white and with large black spots on the forewings, giving an overall greyish appearance in flight. (See p.27)

# Large White

## *Pieris brassicae*

**D**isliked by gardeners because of the voracious appetite of its cater-pillars, the adult Large White is, nevertheless, a lovely butterfly. Its numbers vary from year to year depending on migration from the south but since the heavy use of pesticides in the last 50 years, it is rarely as abundant as it once was. A small parasitic wasp, *Apanteles glomeratus*, also affects the frequency of this butterfly. It lays its eggs in the small caterpillars and the conspicuous yellow cocoons containing the pupae are commonly seen surrounding the dead corpses on walls and fences (see p.13).

Female Large Whites at rest on cabbage leaves, the larval foodplant

| | | | |
|---|---|---|---|
| J | | ♪ | |
| F | | ♪ | |
| M | | ♪ | 🦋 |
| A | • | ♪ | 🦋 |
| M | • | ╱ ♪ | 🦋 |
| J | • | ╱ | 🦋 |
| J | • | ╱ ♪ | 🦋 |
| A | • | ╱ ♪ | 🦋 |
| S | • | ╱ ♪ | 🦋 |
| O | | ╱ ♪ | 🦋 |
| N | | ♪ | |
| D | | ♪ | |

**KEY FEATURES:** The black wing-tips are more extensive than other Whites, with butterflies of the second brood more heavily marked than the first. Males always lack the black spots and streak on the upperside of the forewings. Undersides of both sexes are similar, pale yellow dusted with grey, often heavier in the first brood.

**HABITAT:** Found almost everywhere except high mountains. Commonest in cultivated regions.

**FREQUENCY:** A familiar and common butterfly seen in huge numbers some years after good migrations. Most abundant in July and August.

**LIFE HISTORY:** Large batches of more than 60 yellow eggs are laid (see p.11), usually on the underside of leaves of Brassicas of all kinds, nasturtiums and mignonettes. The caterpillars, which are conspicuous and foul smelling, contain mustard oils to deter predators, though many still succumb to parasites and viral disease (see p.13). Occasionally caterpillars are found as late as December. Pupation may occur well away from the foodplants often in sheds or on walls, the chrysalis is pale green with varying amounts of black spotting depending on the background. Up to three or even four broods may be seen in long hot summers, adult butterflies live for three to four weeks and fly from March until October.

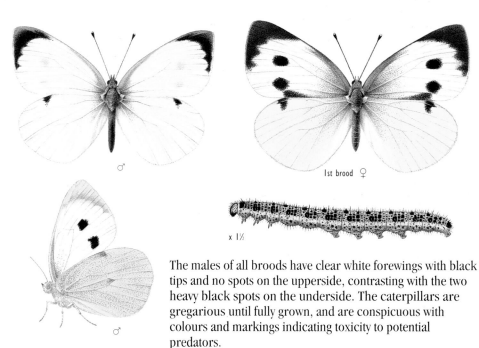

♂

1st brood ♀

x 1½

♂

The males of all broods have clear white forewings with black tips and no spots on the upperside, contrasting with the two heavy black spots on the underside. The caterpillars are gregarious until fully grown, and are conspicuous with colours and markings indicating toxicity to potential predators.

## LOOKALIKES

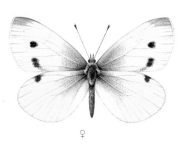

♂

**Small White** *Artogeia rapae*
Usually distinguished by its smaller size. The wing-tip markings are paler and less extensive. Males usually have a black spot on the upperside of the forewing. (See p.32)

**Brimstone**
*Gonepteryx rhamni*
Only the female Brimstone could be confused with the Large White, however it lacks any black markings and apart from its hooked wing-tips, which aren't always apparent in flight, the colour is distinctly greenish-white. It always settles with its wings closed. (See p.44)

♀

♀

# Small White

*Artogeia rapae*

Like its relative the Large White, this common butterfly is best known for the ravages of its caterpillars in the vegetable garden. It is also sometimes mistaken for the Green-veined White with which it often flies and feeds. Despite the attack on its caterpillars from predators and parasites, which kill large numbers, it often appears abundantly, especially so in later generations. At night or in bad weather butterflies can be found at rest amongst the foliage of variegated or pale coloured plants.

1st brood Small Whites feeding from dandelions

♂

1st brood ♂

1st brood ♀

♀

| | | |
|---|---|---|
| J | ❭ | |
| F | ❭ | |
| M | · ❭ | 🦋 |
| A | · ✦❭ | 🦋 |
| M | · ✦❭ | 🦋 |
| J | · ✦❭ | 🦋 |
| J | · ✦❭ | 🦋 |
| A | · ✦❭ | 🦋 |
| S | · ✦❭ | 🦋 |
| O | ✦❭ | 🦋 |
| N | ❭ | |
| D | ❭ | |

**KEY FEATURES:** Less boldly marked and usually smaller than the Large White. Males, especially in the second generation, nearly always have a spot on the upperside of the forewings. The dark wing-tip is always paler and does not extend down the wing edge. Underside of the hindwing is pale yellow with grey dusting and a slightly darker line through the centre of the cell. Summer broods are usually more heavily marked.

**HABITAT:** Ubiquitous, in all types of countryside but especially in towns and gardens.

**FREQUENCY:** Common, from March to October in 2 to 4 broods, most abundant in July and August.

**LIFE HISTORY:** The pale yellow eggs are laid singly on the underside of brassica leaves, both cultivated and wild. Unlike the conspicuous caterpillars of the Large White, it is well camouflaged and most closely resembles the Green-veined White, however the pale dorsal line and two yellow spots on each segment are diagnostic. It feeds for about three weeks then pupates, often on buildings or walls. The chrysalis is similar to but less shiny than the Green-veined White, it varies from pale buff to green and is attached by a silken girdle (see p.15). Hibernation is spent as a chrysalis and the Small White is the first spring-time butterfly to emerge from its chrysalis. Adults live for about three weeks.

2nd brood ♂                                    2nd brood ♀

Males of the first brood often have only very light markings, though females of all broods always have two spots on each forewing. The undersides are similar. The green slightly downy caterpillar has two yellow spots on each segment and a pale dorsal stripe.

x 1½

## LOOKALIKES

♂

♂

**Large White** *Pieris brassicae*
Usually larger with blacker wing-tips and spots, though the male lacks any spotting on the upperside of the forewings. (See p.30)

**Green-veined White** *Artogeia napi*
Similar in size but the veins at the wing margins have dark triangular marks on the upperside. Underside veins are edged with grey-green scales which are usually distinct, though in later broods may be quite faint. Occurs in the same habitats. (See p.34)

♀

**Orange Tip** *Anthocharis cardamines*
The female, which often visits gardens, could be mistaken but its clear black spots and green-marbled underside are characteristic, as is its weaker fluttering flight. (See p.38)

# Green-veined White

*Artogeia napi*

Although the Green-veined White is commonly encountered in cultivated areas, it prefers damp meadows and woodland rides and unlike its two close relatives, its caterpillars are not injurious to garden crops. Its flight is similar to that of the Small White but close examination of the underside of the hindwings will reveal the delicate green-scaled veins. It is one of the earliest springtime butterflies to emerge from its chrysalis though the adults only live for two to three weeks.

Male and female of 2nd brood on lavender

2nd brood ♀

♀

♂

| | | |
|---|---|---|
| J | ♪ | |
| F | ♪ | |
| M | ♪ | |
| A | · ✦ ♪ | 🦋 |
| M | · ✦ ♪ | 🦋 |
| J | · ✦ ♪ | 🦋 |
| J | · ✦ ♪ | 🦋 |
| A | · ✦ ♪ | 🦋 |
| S | · ✦ ♪ | 🦋 |
| O | ✦ ♪ | |
| N | ♪ | |
| D | ♪ | |

**KEY FEATURES:** Ground colour of underside of hindwings and tip of forewings, varying shades of yellow with veins bordered by dark, grey-green scales, those of the second brood being less heavily scaled than the first. Upper forewings, dark scales at the end of the veins forming small triangular marks along wing margins. Both sexes of the second brood are larger and have blacker markings.

**HABITAT:** Found in a wide range of habitats, from flowery, lowland meadows and open woodland rides, to grassy mountain slopes. It is however most often observed in arable and cultivated land.

**FREQUENCY:** Common and sometimes extremely abundant. Occurs throughout the region.

**LIFE HISTORY:** Eggs are laid singly on the underside of leaves of various cruciferous plants, including cuckoo flower, garlic mustard, water cress, hedge mustard and charlock. The caterpillar can be distinguished from that of the Small White by the yellow ringed spiracles along its sides. The chrysalis has two colour forms, green and pale brown and it is in this stage that over-wintering occurs.

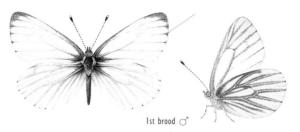

1st brood ♂

1st brood ♀

The black discal spots of the male may be absent in some specimens of the first brood. Females have two spots on each forewing, the lower ones touching the lower margin of the wings. The well camouflaged caterpillar lacks the yellow dorsal stripe of the Small White.

x 1½

## LOOKALIKES

1st brood ♂

**Small White** *Artogeia rapae*
The dark wing-tip markings are less conspicuous and the veins lack the triangular wedges. Undersides lack any scaling along the veins although some darker scales occur towards the base of hindwing. (See p.32)

**Orange Tip** *Anthocharis cardamines*
Only the female could be confused but the black central spot and green marbling, showing from underside of the hindwing, is diagnostic. (See p.38)

1st brood ♀

♀

**Wood White** *Leptidea sinapis*
In damp woodland glades this delicate local butterfly could be confused for a small Green-veined White but its flight is weaker and it always settles with its wings closed. (See p.37)

*35*

# Bath White
*Pontia daplidice*

A rare migrant to northern Europe, the Bath White has recently been split into two distinct species, *Pontia daplidice* and the more easterly, *Pontia edusa* (see *Collins Field Guide Butterflies of Britain and Europe*, HarperCollins*Publishers* 1997). Further south it is a common species often flying with other Whites when identification may be confusing. With practice however, it soon becomes easy to identify the species, especially the female, even in flight, when the black chequering is noticeable.

Eggs are laid on the leaves of wild mignonette and some Crucifers but in Britain and northern Europe the caterpillar is unable to survive the damp, cold winters. The one exception to this is the Scandinavian island of Gotland, where it is resident.

One of the earliest preserved butterflies is a Bath White in the J.C. Dale Collection at Oxford University Museum caught in 1702.

# Peak White
*Pontia callidice*

Much less widely distributed than the Bath White, this Pyrenean and Alpine species reaches just into southern Germany, where it flies in June and July, on grassy mountain slopes over 1,500m.

The black markings on the upperside are finer and more elongate than those of the Bath White and on the underside of the hindwings the pale markings are distinctly V shaped. The caterpillar too is similar but the yellow bands are broken to form rows of spots. It feeds mainly on dwarf treacle mustard.

# Wood White
## *Leptidea sinapsis*

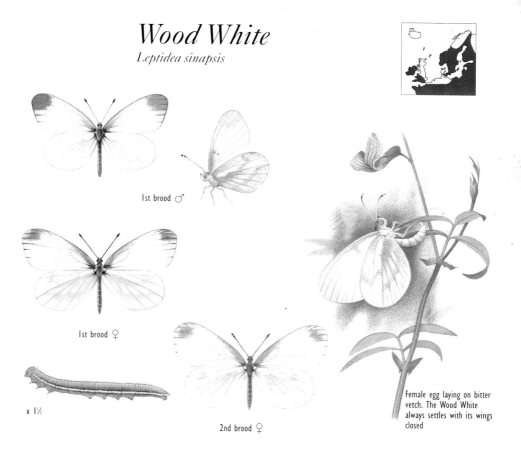

1st brood ♂

1st brood ♀

x 1½

2nd brood ♀

Female egg laying on bitter vetch. The Wood White always settles with its wings closed

The smallest and most delicate of all the Whites, this dainty little butterfly flutters weakly and unhurriedly along woodland glades and meadows, visiting flowers and searching for egg laying sites. The species has recently been split into two on the continent, the other, *Leptidea reali* being found in isolated populations in France, Germany, Belgium and Sweden (see *Collins Field Guide Butterflies of Britain and Europe*, HarperCollinsPublishers 1997).

Various members of the pea family are selected for egg laying, in particular yellow meadow vetchling, tuberous pea, bitter vetch and greater bird's-foot trefoil. The slender camouflaged caterpillar feeds for a month and pupates, producing an elegant yellow pupa similar in shape to the Orange Tip. Those from the second brood over-winter producing the first butterflies the following May. The second brood is on the wing in July and August but in northern Fennoscandia only one brood appears. Local in Britain and northern Europe, further south it is common and may be found in diverse habitats.

| J |
| F |
| M |
| A |
| M |
| J |
| J |
| A |
| S |
| O |
| N |
| D |

# Orange Tip
## *Anthocaris cardamines*

To the butterfly enthusiast, the delightful male Orange Tip is the true harbinger of spring, as it dances its way along country lanes. The female by contrast lacks the orange tips of the male and is often mistaken for the Small White but both sexes have the lovely mottled-green underside, giving marvellous camouflage when they are at rest on the flower heads of umbellifers. Fortunately it is a butterfly that appears to be increasing its range.

Male and female Orange Tips
on periwinkle

J
F
M
A ·
M ·
J ·
J ·
A
S
O
N
D

**KEY FEATURES:** The male is unmistakable, with its bright orange wing-tips. The female which is much less frequently encountered, has grey wing-tips with a clear black central spot on each forewing. The markings from the underside of the hindwings show through faintly to the upperside.

**HABITAT:** Damp meadows, woodland rides and roadside verges, where males patrol in search of females. Also urban and cultivated areas where it is a regular visitor to gardens.

**FREQUENCY:** Never occurring in the huge numbers of some of the other Whites, it is however a familiar insect throughout Europe with an expanding range in the British Isles.

**LIFE HISTORY:** The orange, bottle-shaped egg is easy to find beneath the flower buds of Crucifers, particular favourites being, garlic mustard, cuckoo flower and honesty (see p.10). Isolated plants growing in sunny aspects are chosen, in preference to those growing in dense patches. On hatching, the small caterpillar feeds on developing seed pods but it may also eat other Orange Tip caterpillars it encounters. After three to four weeks, the fully grown caterpillar leaves the foodplant and may wander some distance before pupating amongst dry vegetation. Here the attractive, curved chysalis remains until the following April, perfectly concealed for ten months (see p.14).

x 1½

The beautiful, mossy-green underside which gives perfect camouflage when at rest, contrasts with the brilliant orange and white warning colours of the male. The pale, blue-green caterpillar rests along the seed-pods on which it feeds.

## LOOKALIKES (FEMALE)

There is no mistaking the male Orange Tip but the female may be confused with other members of the White family. However, the central black spot in the centre of the forewings is characteristic.

**Green-veined White**
*Artogeia napi*
Found in similar habitats but stronger in flight, the underside has green-lined veins rather than blotches. It also has a longer flight period than the Orange Tip.
(See p.34)

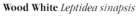

**Small White** *Artogeia rapae*
Less conspicuously marked with black on the forewings and distinguished by the plain underside of the hindwings. (See p.32)

**Wood White** *Leptidea sinapsis*
A local butterfly which may occur in similar places to the Orange Tip but is more feeble in flight and generally smaller. It never alights with its wings open (see p.37)

39

# Clouded Yellow

*Colias croceus*

An irregular visitor to northern Europe from the Mediterranean, the Clouded Yellow sometimes arrives in very large numbers, although this is an increasingly rare happening. Its rich yellow colouring make it a striking sight as it dashes across clover or lucerne fields in late summer. Sadly it is unable to withstand the cold winters of the north in any of its stages.

Clouded Yellow feeding on red clover

f. *helice* ♀

♀

♂

J
F
M
A
M
J
J
A
S
O
N
D

**KEY FEATURES:** The deep marigold-yellow of both sexes is diagnostic, though in south-eastern Germany the Danube Clouded Yellow could be confused. The female, which can occur in a white form *helice*, is slightly darker than the male. The underside of the forewing has a row of bold, black spots decreasing in size towards the apex and on the hindwing there is a white-centred, figure-of-eight mark in the middle.

**HABITAT:** A wanderer through the countryside, found from sea level to hilly regions in diverse habitats where there are plenty of flowers.

**FREQUENCY:** Dependent solely on migrants from the south, usually only a few individuals are recorded each year in northern Europe but some years huge numbers arrive, most recently in 1983 and 1992.

**LIFE HISTORY:** A wide range of leguminous plants are used for egg laying, including lucerne, clovers, trefoils and melilot. The egg is laid on the upper leaf surface and turns from pale yellow to orange. It hatches after about a week and after eating its eggshell the caterpillar spends the following month perfectly camouflaged amongst the leaves of its foodplant. Pupation takes place amongst low vegetation and the butterfly emerges after about eighteen days.

The yellow ground-colour of both sexes varies, particularly in the female, which, in its extreme form occurs as the white form *helice*. The size of the black discal spot and the spots on the underside of the hindwing are also variable. The caterpillar is very similar to the Pale Clouded Yellow which is slightly hairier and more granular in appearance.

x 1½

## LOOKALIKES

All eight Clouded Yellows found in the region settle with their wings closed, so the uppersides are rarely viewed, except in butterfly collections.

### Pale Clouded Yellow
*Colias hyale*
Paler yellow on the uppersides of both sexes but the form *helice* is similar. However *helice* is more heavily marked and the dark markings of the upperside show through when the butterfly settles. (See p. 42)

### Northern Clouded Yellow *Colias hecla*
Upperside ground colour darker orange, underside grey-green with granular appearance. Wing markings, especially the central hindwing spot, less prominent than the Clouded Yellow. A fast flying arctic butterfly occurring in northern Fennoscandia from June to August.

### Danube Clouded Yellow
*Colias myrmidone*
Upperside even brighter than the Clouded Yellow. Black wing borders lack the yellow-lined veins in male, female yellow spots forming continuous bands on hindwings. The dark post discal spots on the underside of the forewings are small or absent. A rare butterfly found from south-eastern Germany eastwards in two broods from May to September.

# Pale Clouded Yellow

*Colias hyale*

An even more irregular visitor to the north than the Clouded Yellow, this butterfly is probably sometimes overlooked, as it can be mistaken for a White or a Brimstone as it flies swiftly over flower rich meadows. It is less strongly migratory than the Clouded Yellow and therefore commoner in continental Europe.

x 1½

♂

♀

The markings of both sexes are similar and very rarely the female occurs with the whitish-green replaced with yellow. The caterpillar is the surest way of distinguishing this species from the Berger's Clouded Yellow.

Male on lucerne, the larval foodplant

| J |   |     |    |
|---|---|-----|----|
| F |   |     |    |
| M |   |     |    |
| A |   |     |    |
| M | · |     | 🦋 |
| J | · | ╱   | 🦋 |
| J | · | ╱ ╲ | 🦋 |
| A | · | ╱ ╲ | 🦋 |
| S | · | ╱ ╲ | 🦋 |
| O | · | ╱ ╲ | 🦋 |
| N |   | ╲   |    |
| D |   |     |    |

**KEY FEATURES:** This and the Berger's Clouded Yellow are notoriously difficult to tell apart, especially the females, however the following features can help in identification:- The Pale Clouded Yellow has more pointed forewings with straighter outer margins. The dark basal dusting on both wings is more extensive, as are the black marginal spots on the hindwings. The male Berger's Clouded Yellow is usually a brighter lemon-yellow and the orange spot in the middle of the hindwing is often more brilliant.

**HABITAT:** Flowery hills and meadows particularly where clover and lucerne is abundant.

**FREQUENCY:** Commoner further south with migrants occasionally reaching southern England and Scandinavia, where it is said to be resident on Gotland.

**LIFE HISTORY:** Eggs are usually laid on lucerne or clovers, though other members of the pea family are sometimes used. The caterpillar is very similar to the Clouded Yellow but it is slightly hairier and more granular. Where this butterfly can survive the cold, wet winters of the north, it does so in this stage. The chrysalis is attached to vegetation by a silken girdle and is unlikely to be found in the wild. Adult butterflies occur in two broods, those of the second being more plentiful.

# LOOKALIKES

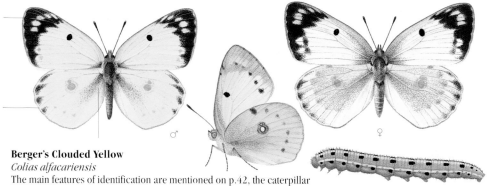

**Berger's Clouded Yellow**
*Colias alfacariensis*
The main features of identification are mentioned on p.42, the caterpillar
being the most reliable means to differentiate the two species. It is green, with two bright
yellow lines with black spots beneath, running down each side. This butterfly is even rarer,
as it is restricted to the distribution of its larval foodplants, the horseshoe vetch and crown
vetch. These are both plants of calcareous soils and it is therefore more likely that this
butterfly will be encountered on scrubby chalk downland, mainly in August and September.

x 1½

**Pale Arctic Clouded Yellow** *Colias nastes*
A true Arctic butterfly, found in northern Fennoscandia,
where it can occur in good numbers from lowlands to
scrubby mountain slopes in May and June. Its colour
varies from pale yellowish-white to greenish-white and
although there is little dusting at the base of the
forewings, the veins are dark. The central spot on both
surfaces of the hindwing is tiny. The caterpillar feeds on
*Vaccinium* species and alpine milk-vetch.

**Mountain Clouded Yellow** *Colias phicomone*
Male with dark suffusion over forewings and both sexes
with clear, pale post-discal markings. Underside of
hindwings orange, with a conspicuous central spot. Flies
from June until August and reaches just into southern
Germany.

**Note.** See also CLOUDED YELLOW *Colias croceus* form
*helice* (see p.40)

**Moorland Clouded Yellow** *Colias palaeno*
A butterfly of damp acidic bogs, from central
Europe, where it is becoming increasingly rare,
to northern Fennoscandia. Its clear, pale wings,
with uninterrupted black borders are distinctive.
It flies from June until August. The caterpillar
feeds on *Vaccinium* species.

*43*

# *Brimstone*

*Gonepteryx rhamni*

The sight of a male Brimstone in early March, having emerged from hibernation, is a welcome sign that spring is on the way. It is one of the longest-lived butterflies, with individuals that hatch in August sometimes surviving until the following July, when they may fly with those of the next generation. In late summer it favours purple and mauve flowers such as teasel, thistle and knapweeds, though yellow flowers, like primrose and daffodil, are often sought in the spring.

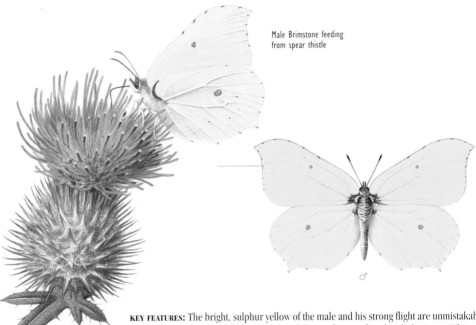

Male Brimstone feeding from spear thistle

♂

**KEY FEATURES:** The bright, sulphur yellow of the male and his strong flight are unmistakable but the female is less easily identified and she is often confused with the Large White. However on closer examination, apart from her hooked wing-tips, her colour is a delicate greenish-white and she lacks any black markings. Brimstones always settle with their wings closed and when at rest, amongst foliage, both sexes are perfectly concealed, especially when hibernating in dense growths of ivy. The underside of the hindwing is greenish-yellow, darker in the male, and the prominent, pale veins resemble the under surface of leaves.

**HABITAT:** Found in woodland rides, on scrubby downland, as well as parks and gardens often well away from the nearest buckthorn bushes.

**FREQUENCY:** A familiar butterfly found throughout Europe apart from the extreme north. It is commonest in July and August, when it can occur in good numbers in woodland rides, feeding with other butterflies on thistles.

**LIFE HISTORY:** Females seek purging buckthorn or alder buckthorn bushes growing in a sunny sheltered position, and lay their eggs on leaves or buds (see p.11). The caterpillar, which rests on the mid-rib of the leaf, feeds for about a month, before turning into a plump leaf-like chrysalis. Adults emerge after about two weeks and often go into hibernation soon afterwards. Mating then occurs the following spring.

J
F
M
A
M
J
J
A
S
O
N
D

Little variation occurs in either sex, though females occasionally appear yellowish. Though well camouflaged, the caterpillar is easy to find, often on very small bushes.

x 1½

## Lookalikes

**Cleopatra** *Gonepteryx cleopatra*
Mainly a butterfly of the Mediterranean and southern Europe but also eastern France. Generally larger than the Brimstone, the male upperside is distinctive and noticeable in flight, but as the butterfly always settles with wings closed identification can be difficult. The main difference is the outer margin of the wings which, in the Cleopatra are straighter and less prominently hooked. Flies from March until August. The caterpillar feeds on various species of buckthorn.

**Pale Clouded Yellow**
*Colias hyale*
Ground colour of the male, and the fact that both species may occur together could confuse at a distance but the Brimstone has no black markings. (See p.42)

*45*

# Brown Hairstreak

*Thecla betulae*

The largest and most beautiful of all our Hairstreaks, it is unfortunate that adults spend much of their lives high in the canopy of large trees, where they have a liking for honeydew, the sugary excretions of aphids. However they do occasionally descend to feed on flowers such as hemp agrimony, thistles and bramble in warm sunshine, and females can be observed egg laying on small blackthorn bushes.

Black Hairstreaks on blackthorn, the larval foodplant

J · 
F · 
M · 
A · 
M · 
J · 
J · 
A · 
S · 
O · 
N · 
D · 

**KEY FEATURES:** The upperside of the male is uniform brown with just a faint pale mark on the forewings and two orange tails. The female is usually larger and more brightly coloured with broad orange bands on the upperside and bolder markings on the under surface.

**HABITAT:** Open woodlands and lanes with large stands of unkempt blackthorn.

**FREQUENCY:** A local butterfly never appearing in very large numbers, found throughout Europe as far north as southern England and Fennoscandia.

**LIFE HISTORY:** The conspicuous white, bun-shaped egg is laid low down on blackthorn twigs and is probably the best way of determining the butterfly's presence (see p.11). They are best searched for in the winter when the leaves have dropped, where they remain until spring. The caterpillar is green with yellow stripes and is well concealed among blackthorn leaves. It feeds until the end of June when it pupates near the ground. The butterfly emerges after three to four weeks with peak numbers in early September. Individuals live for about three weeks.

Of all the blackthorn feeding Hairstreaks only the Brown Hairstreak is able to bask with its wings open. At rest the caterpillar remains concealed on the underside of leaves.

## LOOKALIKES

x 2¼

### Sloe Hairstreak *Satyrium acaciae*

This butterfly and its life history resembles that of the Black Hairstreak but the upper surface usually has less orange and the male lacks the sex-brands. Females have a characteristic black tip to the abdomen, these are hairs that are used to conceal the eggs which over-winter on blackthorn twigs. It flies in central and eastern Europe but is absent from Britain and Scandinavia, it is found in open scrubby areas where it feeds on flowers such as yarrow. Single brooded it appears in June and July.

### Black Hairstreak *Satyrium pruni*

Found in similar habitats but is more restricted in its distribution especially in north-western Europe. Absent from north and western France and all but the southern edge of Fennoscandia but local in central England. It is smaller and darker than the Brown Hairstreak and the orange is confined to the outer margins of the wings. On the underside of the hindwing the black tear-drop shaped spots that border the tapering orange band are diagnostic. The upper forewings of the male have a small, grey sex-brand near the front margin but this is impossible to see in the wild as they always settle with their wings shut. The caterpillar, which feeds on the buds and leaves of blackthorn, is green with pairs of faint pink spots along its back. It pupates attached to twigs and the chrysalis, though resembling a bird dropping, nevertheless often falls prey to insectivorous birds (see p.14). This butterfly has a short flight period lasting from the last week of June to mid-July.

Tip of female's abdomen

# Purple Hairstreak

*Quercusia quercus*

The commonest of the Hairstreaks, often appearing in very large numbers, the Purple Hairstreak is nevertheless an elusive butterfly to observe at close hand, as it rarely visits flowers, preferring to feed on honeydew high in the canopy of ash and oak trees. Males congregate together and their presence can be detected by lobbing a small pebble high into the upper branches, causing them to fly out to inspect the object in the hope that it is a female.

Female Purple Hairstreaks
on common oak

**KEY FEATURES:** In flight, high up in the tree tops, this butterfly may look almost black but the male has a beautiful purple sheen with dark borders on the upperside. The female has reduced but brighter purple markings, though the undersides of both sexes are similar. Occasionally this butterfly can be seen basking on the foliage of oak trees.

**HABITAT:** Mixed woodland and scrubby areas containing oak and ash, though colonies may also occur on isolated oaks in hedgerows or gardens.

**FREQUENCY:** Found throughout the region, except the far north, sometimes appearing in large numbers.

**LIFE HISTORY:** The eggs are laid beneath the buds of oak twigs in warm, sheltered positions. They hibernate until the following March when the young caterpillars emerge and start to feed within the leaf-bud. The fully grown caterpillar feeds and rests on the expanding buds and is beautifully camouflaged amongst the bracts, which it spins together to form a shelter. It lives for about six weeks and then changes into a plump brown chrysalis which is capable of making a rasping squeak (see p.15). After a month the adult butterfly emerges, the first appearing in late June in one generation lasting until September.

J
F
M
A
M
J
J
A
S
O
N
D

The sexes are distinctive on the uppersides but the undersides are very similar, however the male is usually slightly larger than the female. Just before pupation the caterpillar changes from ochreous-brown to dull, lilac-olive.

x 2¼

## LOOKALIKES

**Ilex Hairstreak** *Satyrium ilicis*
Commoner further south in continental Europe, rare in southern Fennoscandia and absent from Britain. This butterfly flies from June until August amongst oaks growing on warm open hillsides and woodland glades. The caterpillar is bright yellow-green and like the Purple Hairstreak, it feeds on various species of oak.

**Green Hairstreak** *Callophrys rubi*
A distinctive little butterfly that always settles with its wings closed, showing its green underside, unique amongst butterflies of northern Europe. It is widespread and generally common, though rarely occurs in large numbers. It is often overlooked as much of its time is spent perching on vegetation. It has a wide range of larval foodplants, including, gorse, bilberry, dogwood, bramble, buckthorn, broom, rock-rose and various members of the pea family such as bird's foot trefoil and vetches. The sluggish green and yellow caterpillar will also cannibalise others of its species it encounters. Pupation usually takes place near the ground beneath moss or leaves and here the chrysalis remains until the following spring. The first butterflies can be seen in April in one generation that lasts until July. The male has a small grey sex-brand on each forewing, otherwise the sexes are identical. The main variation is in the boldness of the white spots on the underside.

x 2¼

# White-letter Hairstreak

*Satyrium w-album*

Awidespread but always local butterfly, the White-letter Hairstreak suffered a serious decline following the ravages of Dutch-elm disease. However it managed to hang on and its numbers now seem to be increasing, with young elm suckers being used as egg laying sites rather than large mature trees formerly used. Like many of the other Hairstreaks much time is spent high in the canopy of large trees but they often descend to feed from flowers, favouring thistles and bramble.

White-letter Hairstreaks feeding from creeping thistle

J •
F •
M •
A • /
M / )
J ) 🦋
J • ) 🦋
A • 🦋
S •
O •
N •
D •

**KEY FEATURES:** The upperside of both sexes is dark brown with the male having a sex-brand on each forewing, though this feature is seldom seen as they always settle with wings closed. The underside is usually slightly paler in the female but the longer tail of her hindwings is the easiest way of distinguishing the sexes. The white 'W' on the hindwings from where the butterfly gets its name, is variable in its boldness and very rarely is it absent

**HABITAT:** Colonies are often restricted to just one large tree either in mature deciduous woodlands or in hedgerows.

**FREQUENCY:** A local butterfly whose numbers have gradually increased in the last twenty years since Dutch-elm disease. Although colonies are often overlooked, numbers can get very high.

**LIFE HISTORY:** The unique button-shaped egg is laid in a fork near the base of a leaf bud on common elm or more frequently wych elm. Here it remains until the following spring when the caterpillar emerges to feed on the developing leaf buds. When fully grown, after about six weeks, it matches perfectly the elm leaves on which it feeds and rests. It pupates either on a leaf or twig of the foodplant and remains there for three to four weeks until the first butterflies appear in June. There is one generation a year with individuals living for about three weeks.

Males are almost black when freshly emerged with females only slightly paler and with noticeably longer hindwing tails. The caterpillar is usually a clear greenish-yellow but sometimes has pale pinkish markings on some segments.

x 2⅓

## LOOKALIKES

**Black Hairstreak** *Satyrium pruni*
Upperside orange marginal markings on hindwings and sometimes on forewings. Underside brighter with more orange and conspicuous black spots, the white streaks lack the clear 'W'. (See p.47)

**Sloe Hairstreak** *Satyrium acaciae*
Northern limit similar to the Blue-spot Hairstreak, this butterfly is one of the smallest of the Hairstreaks, with quite pale markings on the underside. The female can be identified by the black tuft of hairs at the tip of the abdomen. (See p.47)

**Blue-spot Hairstreak** *Satyrium spini*
Absent from Britain and northern Europe this butterfly occurs in open, scrubby woodland where buckthorn and blackthorn, the larval foodplants grow. The upperside resembles the White-letter Hairstreak but for an orange spot near the tail and the female sometimes has a slight orange flush on her forewings. The white streak on the underside is quite straight and where it meets the orange band, near the tail, there is a patch of pale blue scales, which may be reduced in some specimens. It occurs in a single generation from June until August.

# Small Copper

*Lycaena phlaeas*

A delightful, lively little butterfly, whose male aggressively defends his territory, darting out at any intruding insects, regardless of size. Returning to his perch he sits with wings half open to await the next encounter. Although a common and widespread butterfly throughout Europe, it can be seen in a wide variety of habitats, though usually only in small numbers.

Small Coppers feeding on fleabane

♀

♂

Male perching ready to
defend his territory

| | | |
|---|---|---|
| J | ✒ | |
| F | ✒ | |
| M | ✒ | |
| A | ✒ ✑ | ✹ |
| M · | ✒ ✑ | ✹ |
| J · | ✒ ✑ | ✹ |
| J · | ✒ ✑ | ✹ |
| A · | ✒ ✑ | ✹ |
| S · | ✒ ✑ | ✹ |
| O · | ✒ ✑ | ✹ |
| N | ✒ | |
| D | ✒ | |

**KEY FEATURES:** With its clear, brilliant copper forewings, spotted with black, the Small Copper is unmistakable, especially in Britain where the only other Copper is the very rare, Large Copper, which is restricted to its last remaining site in Cambridgeshire. In northern Fennoscandia sub-species *polaris* occurs. It has a paler, more variegated underside with bolder black spots and appears in just one generation.

**HABITAT:** Even the most unpromising waste-ground and barren roadside verges, as well as unspoilt downland meadows, woodland rides, heaths and gardens.

**FREQUENCY:** A common, sun-loving butterfly, found throughout the summer from April to October.

**LIFE HISTORY:** The egg, which is like a minute, flattened golf ball, is laid on leaves of sorrel and docks. The young caterpillar feeds on the leaf cuticle making conspicuous opaque windows which form channels all over the leaves. When fully grown it is green and slug like, sometimes with pink stripes lining the body. Those of the final brood hibernate until the following spring. The plump greenish-brown chrysalis, which is unlikely to be found in the wild, lasts for about a month.

L. p. polaris ♀

The male is often smaller than the female with more pointed forewings, specimens of later generations are often larger and brighter. Extreme aberrations are rare, though specimens with silvery-blue spots on the hindwings, f. *caeruleopunctata*, are frequent. The fully grown caterpillar can sometimes be found on the underside of leaves close to the ground.

## LOOKALIKES

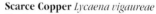

**Violet Copper** *Lycaena helle*
A beautiful little butterfly which is found in widely scattered colonies throughout Europe but which is endangered in some regions due to loss of habitat. It occurs, sometimes commonly, in damp, boggy areas, open woodlands and warm, flowery meadows. There is much variation amongst individuals, those in the north being generally darker. The caterpillar feeds on bistort or sorrel in one generation a year, the butterfly flying in May and June. Absent from Britain.

**Sooty Copper** *Lycaena tityrus*
The common name refers mainly to the male, though the female too, is more dusky than the Small Copper. The underside of both sexes is greenish-yellow with strong black spotting, giving an ochreous appearance in flight. The caterpillar feeds on sorrel usually in two generations and the butterfly appears from April to September. It flies in a variety of sheltered, flowery habitats throughout most of continental Europe but is absent from Britain and most of Fennoscandia.

**Scarce Copper** *Lycaena vigaureae*
The female of this butterfly, particularly f. *oranulus* which flies in northern Fennoscandia could be confused with the Small Copper but the white markings on the underside of the hindwings are distinctive. (See p.55)

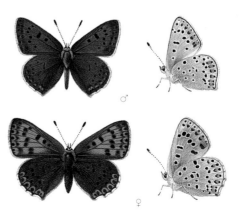

# Large Copper
### *Lycaena dispar*

Alovely butterfly, sadly threatened with extinction in some localities, through drainage of its wetland habitats. It is an active, sun-loving insect with a liking for damp flower-rich meadows. During the last century it was prized amongst butterfly collectors in England, whose activities along with fenland drainage, may have contributed to its demise. However the re-introduction of continental stock, sub-species *batava*, earlier this century has allowed this butterfly a tenuous foothold in Britain.

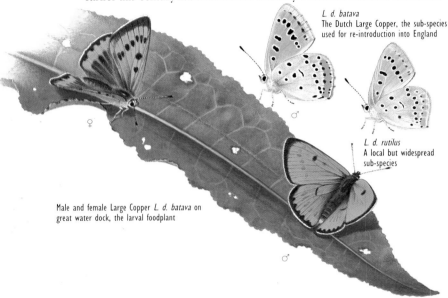

L. d. batava
The Dutch Large Copper, the sub-species used for re-introduction into England

♂

L. d. rutilus
A local but widespread sub-species

Male and female Large Copper *L. d. batava* on great water dock, the larval foodplant

♀

♂

J ✦
F ✦
M ✦
A ✦
M ✦ ♪
J · ✦ ♪ 🦋
J · ✦ ♪ 🦋
A · ✦ ♪ 🦋
S ✦
O ✦
N ✦
D ✦

**KEY FEATURES:** The male has clear, brilliant orange wings with black borders and a black spot at the centre of each wing, bolder on the forewings. The female is heavily spotted with black and resembles the females of some other Coppers but the delicate blue and orange of the undersides of both sexes is diagnostic. Various sub-species occur throughout Europe with the extinct English sub-species *dispar* being regarded as the most magnificent.

**HABITAT:** In England a fenland butterfly restricted to Woodwalton Fen in Cambridgeshire but elsewhere in Europe it frequents marshy areas, dykes and wet meadows.

**FREQUENCY:** A local butterfly found in widely scattered colonies throughout Europe but absent from Fennoscandia.

**LIFE HISTORY:** The caterpillar feeds on great water dock in Britain and on other species of wetland docks elsewhere. It is a clear green when young but changes to dull lilac before hibernation, which takes place amongst withered leaves, here it may be completely submerged for several months in the winter. Feeding starts again in the spring when the caterpillar regains its green coloration. Those that survive the ordeal pupate on reed stems and the first butterflies appear after about two weeks in a single generation in England and Holland and two generations elsewhere, between June and August.

x 1½

The flame-orange of the male with a black spot and sometimes an additional smaller one, on each forewing is diagnostic. Though similar to other females the Large Copper is generally bigger. Caterpillars that produce a second generation live for about three weeks, whereas those of the ssp *batava* may live for up to ten months.

## LOOKALIKES

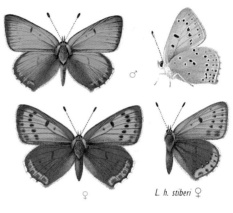

f. *oranulus* Lapland ♂

L. h. *stiberi* ♀

**Scarce Copper** *Lycaena vigaureae*
The male lacks the black spots of the forewings. The female is more heavily spotted and lacks the clear, broad orange band of the hindwing. The irregular white spots on the underside of the hindwings are diagnostic. In Lapland the form *oranulus* is smaller and more yellow. More widely distributed than the Large Copper, this active butterfly occurs in damp, flowery meadows where its larval foodplants, sorrel and docks grow. It flies in one generation in July and August.

**Purple-edged Copper** *Lycaena hippothoe*
Found throughout Fennoscandia, central France and eastern Europe. The typical male has deep red wings with dark purple margins. The female is duller with a curved band of elongated black spots on the forewings. In northern Fennoscandia sub-species *stiberi* is paler orange. This butterfly flies in June and July in damp meadows from coastal regions to flowery mountain slopes. The caterpillar feeds on bistort and sorrel.

**Purple Shot Copper** *Lycaena alciphron*
An attractive and variable butterfly with males of some sub-species in the south brightly suffused with purple. In the north males are more smokily suffused and the females are mainly brown. The underside of the hind-wing has a clear, orange marginal band, similar to the sooty copper but with the ground-colour less greenish-yellow. It flies in sunny, flowery places in June and July and is a local insect that is absent from north western Europe. The early stages resemble other Coppers, the caterpillar feeding on sorrel.

# Long-tailed Blue

*Lampides boeticus*

This butterfly has a huge distributional range worldwide, including, Africa, Asia, Australia and the Pacific Islands. In Europe though, it is resident only in the Mediterranean region, with migrants spreading north and only rarely reaching as far as southern Britain. It is a sun lover with a quick, jerky flight and is sometimes mistaken for the blue form of the female Common Blue.

Long-tailed Blues feeding on bramble flowers

x 2¼

The colour of the caterpillar ranges from bright green to dull ochreous

J
F
M
A
M
J
J
A
S
O
N
D

**KEY FEATURES:** Variable in size, the male is dull purple with a granular hairy upperside, made up of adroconial scales. The female is darker with purplish-blue forewings and both sexes have two characteristic black spots and a slender tail on the hindwings. Undersides of the sexes are similar, pale brown, striped with white and the black spot near the tail has a silvery-blue centre. From a distance the most distinctive feature is the broad white band across the underside of the hindwing when the butterfly is at rest.

**HABITAT:** Found in many habitats including cultivated areas, scrubby meadows and warm flowery hillsides.

**FREQUENCY:** Can be very common where it is resident in the south but becomes increasingly scarce and very rare in the north.

**LIFE HISTORY:** The eggs are laid on the flower buds of various members of the pea family, including cultivated peas and beans but with a preference in the wild for bladder senna. On hatching the young caterpillar burrows into the developing buds and pods and remains concealed until fully grown. Pupation is amongst dried leaves and lasts for about ten days. Butterflies are usually recorded in July and August in the north but in some warmer countries it can occur in any month, as it is continuously brooded, with no hibernating period. For this reason it is unable to survive anywhere other than in warm climates.

The size of specimens is variable with sometimes very small individuals commonly occurring. The intensity of the purple ground colour of both sexes is variable.

## LOOKALIKES

**Lang's Short-tailed Blue** *Leptotes pirithous*
Smaller, with a brighter purple upperside in the male, both sexes have less conspicuous spots near the tail. On the underside the markings are more mottled and there is no broad white band on the hindwing. Scarcer, with a more southerly distribution than the Long-tailed Blue, migrants rarely get further north than central France and southern Germany. It is continuously brooded in the Mediterranean, the caterpillar feeds on various members of the pea family.

**Short-tailed Blue** *Everes argiades*
As its name implies, the tails of this butterfly are much shorter than those of the other 'tailed Blues'. The male is a fairly constant violet-blue but the amount of violet in the female is variable. The underside is diagnostic with the distinctive orange and black spots near the tail. Flies from April until August, mainly in central and southern Europe, very rare in the north. The caterpillar feeds on bird's foot trefoil, clovers and other Legumes.

**Common Blue** *Polyommatus icarus*
Similar in flight to the Long-tailed Blue, the two species are sometimes confused but closer inspection should easily separate them. (See p.74)

blue ♀

# Small Blue

*Cupido minimus*

The tiniest and most delicate of our butterflies, the Small Blue is a charming though undistinguished little insect that often goes unnoticed. Colonies may be restricted to small isolated areas of roadside verge with only a few individuals but in some places many hundreds may fly in good years. They usually fly close to the ground and as well as visiting a variety of flowers, also feed on moist ground and even on perspiring human skin.

Butterflies often feed on damp ground where mineral salts are obtained

Male Small Blues on the flowers of kidney vetch the caterpillars' foodplant

| | | |
|---|---|---|
| J | / | |
| F | / | |
| M | / | |
| A | / ♪ | |
| M | · ♪ | 🦋 |
| J | · / | 🦋 |
| J | · / | 🦋 |
| A | / ♪ | 🦋 |
| S | / | 🦋 |
| O | / | |
| N | / | |
| D | / | |

**KEY FEATURES:** The uppersides of both sexes are similar though the male has a dusting of silvery-blue scales near the body. Its flight is weak as it flits from flower to flower though it is capable of more rapid dashes, when it can be mistaken for a Brown Argus. Males often bask on vegetation with wings half open but when the butterfly is resting with its wings closed it resembles a small, dull Holly Blue for which it is sometimes mistaken.

**HABITAT:** Dry, sheltered limestone and chalk downland where kidney vetch grows, as well as road verges and railway embankments.

**FREQUENCY:** A common and widely distributed butterfly but quite local in Britain, restricted to the occurrence of its larval foodplant.

**LIFE HISTORY:** The eggs are laid singly amongst the woolly calyxes of the kidney vetch flowerheads, the only foodplant of the caterpillar. When young, the caterpillar feeds inside the calyx on the developing seeds but will also devour any other Small Blues it may encounter. Larger caterpillars feed and rest on the outer seed cases where, although well camouflaged, they are easy to find (see p.12). The fully grown caterpillar then finds a sheltered place close to the ground to pupate but those that do not produce a second brood, remain there until the following spring and pupate in April. The chrysalis is buff with a row of black spots along each side, it lives for about two weeks before the first butterflies emerge in May. In the north of its range a single generation is produced but in warm years and further south two may occur.

There is some variation in the size of individuals and also in the amount of spotting on the underside of the wings. Caterpillars rest, head downwards, on dried seedheads (see p.12), and are pale buff though some may be tinged with green or yellow.

x 2¼

## LOOKALIKES

**Osiris Blue** *Cupido osiris*
Occurs mainly in the Mediterranean and Balkan regions but just reaches as far north as the French border with south-western Germany. This butterfly resembles a small Mazarine Blue, though the row of spots on the underside of the forewings is closer to the wing margins. It flies in warm flowery places, often on mountain sides, where its larval foodplant, sainfoin grows. It may appear in one or two broods and flies from May to September.

**Holly Blue** *Celastrina argiolus*
Larger than the Small Blue but with a similar underside. However the ground colour is more silvery-blue. May occur in the same habitat. (See p.60)

**Short-tailed Blue** *Everes argiades*
The darker female especially could be confused in flight with the Small Blue but the underside has characteristic orange spots and a fine tail on the hindwings. (See p.57)

**Mazarine Blue** *Cyaniris semiargus*
A larger butterfly, the underside is similar but slightly darker. It has more blue at the base and the row of spots on the forewings is further from the margins. (See p.68)

# Holly Blue
*Celastrina argiolus*

A familiar butterfly most years in parks and gardens, the Holly Blue is often referred to as the Common Blue by the less-well informed. Some years however it can be rather scarce, due perhaps to climatic fluctuations but also to the abundance of a parasitic wasp which preys solely upon the caterpillars of the Holly Blue.

2nd brood ♀

Butterflies of the second brood lay their eggs mainly on the flower buds of ivy

J ♪
F ♪
M ♪ 🦋
A · ♪ 🦋
M · ⁄ 🦋
J · ⁄♪ 🦋
J · ⁄♪ 🦋
A · ⁄♪ 🦋
S ⁄♪ 🦋
O ♪
N ♪
D ♪

**KEY FEATURES:** The lilac-blue wings of the male have thin black borders, slightly bolder near the tip of the forewings and the white fringes are distinctly chequered with black. The upperside of the female is unmistakable with her broad black bands, especially heavy in the second generation. The underside of both sexes is similar, a delicate silvery-blue ground colour, finely speckled with black and no trace of orange. Unlike most blues the Holly Blue is frequently seen flying high up around trees and shrubs.

**HABITAT:** Open woodland glades, shrubby areas, parks and gardens with good growths of evergreens such as holly and ivy. As well as feeding on nectar, butterflies can often be seen drinking on damp patches of mud and from sap exuding from tree wounds.

**FREQUENCY:** Common most years, this is the most frequently seen Blue in cultivated places. It is found throughout Europe except the extreme north.

**LIFE HISTORY:** Holly is the usual larval foodplant in the spring but the summer brood favours the flower buds of ivy, however many other plants have been recorded, including, dogwood, buckthorn, gorse, bramble, heathers and pyracantha. The caterpillar is variable in colour but usually pale green, it feeds for three to four weeks before turning a dirty pink in preparation for pupation which often occurs some distance from its feeding area. Pupation takes place secreted behind bark, where those of the second brood remain for about six months. It is one of the first butterflies to appear in the spring, from late March in warm years, with butterflies from the summer brood lasting into September.

1st brood ♀

x 2¼

Males of both generations are identical but the second brood females are darker purple with broader black margins. Caterpillars are easiest to find in August feeding on the developing flower buds of ivy.

## LOOKALIKES

**Small Blue** *Cupido minimus*
The underside of the Small Blue is similar but greyer and butterflies are usually much smaller. (See p.58)

**Common Blue** *Polyommatus icarus*
May fly in the same habitats as the Holly Blue, often in cultivated areas, distinguished by the more colourful and heavily spotted underside and by the clear, white, wing fringes. (See p.74)

**Short-tailed Blue** *Everes argiades*
Underside similar but fine tail and orange spots on the hindwings are diagnostic. (See p.57)

**Green-underside Blue** *Glaucopsyche alexis*
A common butterfly in central Europe but absent from Britain and northern Fennoscandia. It is less violet than the Holly Blue with the black borders of the male generally wider and the white fringes unbroken by black. The female has much less blue, often being completely brown. The underside of the hindwings has a greenish-yellow flush at the base, with small black spots which are sometimes absent. On the forewings however the spots are prominent. Found on warm flowery slopes, woodland edges and clearings where the larval food-plants, milk vetch, medick, broom and other Legumes grow. It flies from April until July in a single generation.

**Mazarine Blue** *Cyaniris semiargus*
The uppersides of both sexes are distinctive but the undersides resemble very large specimens of the Small Blue, however the Mazarine Blue is darker with a noticeable blue basal flush. Extinct in Britain. (See p.68)

*61*

# Large Blue
## *Maculinea arion*

Prized amongst English butterfly collectors of the last century, the Large Blue declined and eventually became extinct in Britain in 1979, due partly to over-collecting in some places and agricultural changes elsewhere. The five European 'Large Blue' species are unique in that their caterpillars live in symbiosis with ants, feeding solely upon their larvae in their later stages.

Large Blues on thyme

The fat, grub like caterpillar lives underground and so is rarely seen

x 2¼

| | |
|---|---|
| J | ✓ |
| F | ✓ |
| M | ✓ |
| A | ✓ |
| M | ✓ ◗ |
| J | • ◗ 🦋 |
| J | • ✓ ◗ 🦋 |
| A | • ✓ |
| S | ✓ |
| O | ✓ |
| N | ✓ |
| D | ✓ |

**KEY FEATURES:** The bright shining blue uppersides of both sexes are similar, though the female may often be larger with bolder black spots. Specimens at higher altitude tend to be generally darker. The underside is ochreous-buff with heavier spotting than other 'Large Blues'. Silvery-blue or green scales are also usually present at the base of the wings. Its flight is generally slow but it is capable of more rapid bursts when alarmed, and in dull weather it takes shelter in gorse or heather.

**HABITAT:** Warm, scrubby hillsides and valleys, coastal areas and forest clearings.

**FREQUENCY:** Local and endangered in some parts of northern Europe, where, in southern England, it has been re-introduced into several sites. Further south it is more secure and can be locally common, particularly in mountainous areas of central Europe.

**LIFE HISTORY:** The egg is laid singly on flowerheads of thyme and after hatching the young caterpillar feeds within the florets on the developing seeds. During its early life, like some other Blues it is cannibalistic but this ceases after its last moult and an even more remarkable life-style ensues. After dropping to the ground, the still small caterpillar exudes a sugary liquid which is eagerly sought by ants, they then adopt it and take it to their nest (see p.13). Here it remains until the following June, having become bloated on a diet of ant larvae. It pupates still in the ants' nest chamber and remains as a chrysalis a further three weeks before hatching, a subterranean life of about ten months. Flies in June and July in a single brood.

Great variation can occur on the upperside of the female, particularly in the size of the spots and the amount of dark suffusion which may obscure most of the blue. The size of the butterfly also varies with dwarf specimens not uncommon.

## LOOKALIKES

The Large Blue *M. Arion* is the most widespread of the *Maculinea* species, though all five are declining and are regarded as vulnerable.

**Mountain Alcon Blue** *Maculinea rebeli*
Once regarded as a sub-species of the Alcon Blue, the male is brighter, with slightly broader margins, the female also has more blue. It often occurs in drier and higher altitudes in central France and southern Germany, eastwards.

**Alcon Blue** *Maculinea alcon*
The male is dull violet-blue with narrow dark margins. Females are more variable, often with very little blue and obscure dark spots. Underside is greyish-buff with small spots, much weaker than the Large Blue. It is a butterfly of wet meadows where it flies in June and July. Although its life-cycle is similar to the other Large Blue, its caterpillars feed on gentians and are adopted by different species of ant. Found throughout central Europe, absent from Britain and northern Fennoscandia.

**Scarce Large Blue** *Maculinea telejus*
Male pale silvery-blue, noticeably lighter near the outer margins where the veins are prominent. Female with broad dark borders, underside of both sexes pale brown with central band of spots bold and no blue scales at the base. The caterpillar feeds on great burnet in its early stages. Rare in southern Germany, eastwards.

**Dusky Large Blue** *Maculinea nausithous*
Both sexes heavily suffused with dark brown, the female usually without blue flush. Wing-fringes are characteristically buff and the underside dusky-buff with no marginal markings. The caterpillar feeds on great burnet in its early stages. Flies in June and July. Very rare in southern Germany and eastern France.

# Silver-studded Blue

*Plebejus argus*

A widespread butterfly whose female is particularly variable, ranging from predominantly blue, to brown. It can be locally abundant when many hundreds may be found roosting communally or basking in the morning sunshine. The name comes from the black marginal spots on the underside of the hindwings which are studded with silvery-blue centres. These also occur on the Idas and Reverdin's Blue.

ssp. *caernensis* ♀
North Wales

x 2¼

Gorse is one of the many larval foodplants

The caterpillar is clear green with a distinctive purple dorsal stripe

J
F
M
A
M
J
J
A
S
O
N
D

**KEY FEATURES:** The male has deep violet-blue wings with broad black margins and the female, which has varying amounts of blue, usually has a series of orange crescents on the hindwings, sometimes extending into the forewings. Males of this species have a small spine at the end of the tibia of the front legs. This is absent in the Idas Blue.

**HABITAT:** Occurs in diverse habitats from sea level to mountain slopes. In Britain it is found mainly on acid heaths and more rarely on limestone and chalk downland.

**FREQUENCY:** A widespread butterfly, locally common, though sometimes appearing in very large numbers.

**LIFE HISTORY:** A wide range of plants are used for egg-laying including gorse, broom, heathers, bird's foot trefoil and rock-rose. The white eggs are laid singly and over-winter until March (see p.10). On hatching the caterpillar feeds on young, tender growth and reaches full-size after about three months. It then pupates below ground in association with ants and the butterflies emerge after a further two to three weeks. A single brood is produced in the north and two further south, flying from June to August. Ssp. *caernensis*, from north Wales, is unusual, in that it appears two to three weeks earlier than other British sub-species.

# LOOKALIKES

**Baton Blue** *Pseudophilotes baton*

**Eastern Baton Blue** *Pseudophilotes vicrama*

**Baton Blue** *Pseudophilotes baton*
A small powdery, blue-grey butterfly with clearly chequered wing fringes and a female with wings heavily suffused with brown. The underside of the hindwings are boldly spotted and have orange bands that lack silver-studs. Flies in dry warm places throughout central Europe.

**Eastern Baton Blue** *Pseudophilotes vicrama*
A very similar butterfly and once regarded as a sub-species of the Baton Blue but with a more easterly distribution. It is usually slightly larger with bolder markings on the underside.

**Chequered Blue** *Scolitantides orion*
Like a large, heavily marked Baton Blue, strongly chequered on the underside. The blue on the upperside is variable with northern specimens tending to be brighter. Found in two separate populations in southern Europe and southern Fennoscandia. It flies in May and June over rocky terrain, where its larval foodplant, white sedum grows.

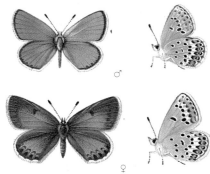

**Idas Blue** *Plebejus idas*
The male lacks a tibial spine and is a brighter, violet-blue with narrow, black borders. The female has distinct orange lunules and the wings often have a heavy suffusion of purple, usually with some buff in the fringes. It is the commonest and most widespread of the three *Plebejus* species and is found throughout Europe except the extreme south and Britain.

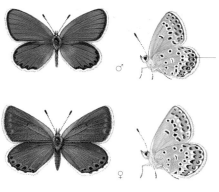

**Reverdin's Blue** *Plebejus argyrognomon*
The wings of the male are clear, deep blue, with narrow borders. The amount of blue on the female is variable but the fringes of her wings are noticeably white. The underside of both sexes is more uniform, without the conspicuous, ragged white band, much paler in Scandinavia. Found in eastern France, southern Germany and scattered colonies northward to southern Scandinavia.

65

# Brown Argus

*Aricia agestis*

An attractive butterfly, fond of basking in warm sunshine but whose rapid, flickery flight may cause it to be over-looked. It often roosts communally, head down amongst grasses, sometimes with Common Blues with which it may be mistaken. The sexes are similar and there is no trace of blue on either surface.

♂          ♀

As well as bolder, orange spots on the forewings, females are larger with more rounded wings

x 2¼

The caterpillar is almost identical to that of the Northern Brown Argus

**KEY FEATURES:** Chocolate brown uppersides with orange marginal lunules in both sexes, sometimes almost absent on the forewings of the male but bold and reaching the wing-tips in females. The underside of the female is slightly browner. The *Aricias* can be separated from other Blues by the almost vertical twin spots on the top-edge of the hindwing and by the absence of a spot in the cell of the forewing. In flight, the silver-grey appearance contrasts with the blue-grey of the female Common Blue. There may be some slight chequering in the wing fringes.

**HABITAT:** Favours warm, flowery hillsides on limestone and chalk downland, sometimes on heathland and open woodland rides.

**FREQUENCY:** Locally common not often occurring in large numbers, found throughout Europe except northern Fennoscandia and northern Britain.

**LIFE HISTORY:** The egg is laid on the underside of the leaves of rock-rose or storks-bill and here the young caterpillar feeds, producing conspicuous opaque windows. Those from the second brood hibernate and when fully grown are green with pale pink and white stripes along the sides. Like other Blues they are attractive to ants. The pale olive-green chrysalis is formed near the ground and lasts for about two weeks. Butterflies of the first generation emerge in May, those of the second in July, until September.

# LOOKALIKES

A. a. allous ♂

x 2¼

**Northern Brown Argus** *Aricia atraxerxes*
In Scotland this butterfly is easily identified by the reduced orange bands, the conspicuous white spots on the forewings, and on the underside, by the small, or absent black centres to the white spots. In northern England however, these features are reversed in sub-species *salmacis*, which resembles the continental and Scandinavian sub-species *allous*. This lacks the white spots on the upperwings and has a fully-spotted under-surface. Butterflies appear in a single generation from June until early August and although the early stages are similar to the Brown Argus, the eggs are laid on the upper surface of the larval foodplant.

**Geranium Argus** *Eumedonia eumedon*
A rather plain butterfly which flies locally in diverse flower-rich habitats, mainly in north-eastern Europe. The white wing fringes are conspicuous and the pale streak from the centre of the underside of the hindwing is diagnostic. In the extreme north it is smaller with reduced markings on the underside. It flies in a single generation in June and July where various geraniums, its larval foodplants, grow.

**Silvery Argus** *Pseudaricia nicias*
Upperside of male, silvery blue, with wide dark borders and a central spot on the forewings, female plain brown with feint central spots. The undersides of both sexes are pale grey with a diagnostic white streak through the centre, towards the body. An uncommon butterfly, which flies in warm, flowery meadows and woodland clearings in eastern Sweden and southern Finland. Single brooded it flies in July and August. Its caterpillar feeds on meadow cranesbill.

**Common Blue** *Polyommatus icarus*
The female Common Blue is often mistaken for the Brown Argus but even females of the brown form have some blue hairs and scales near the body and around the margins of the hindwings. On the underside of the hindwing, the row of spots between the orange band and the central spot, form a clean curve, compared to the displaced twin spots of the Brown Argus. The underside of the forewing has a spot in the cell. (See p.74)

**Silver-studded Blue** *Plebejus argus*
The female is similar but usually has at least, a dusting of blue scales, with the orange markings crescent shaped and duller. (See p.64)

# Mazarine Blue

*Cyaniris semiargus*

Extinct in Britain, with only a few records this century, the Mazarine Blue is still a fairly common butterfly further south, where it flies in damp uncultivated meadows with an abundance of red clover, its larval foodplant. It has a strong flight and between visits to a variety of flowers, spends much of its time basking in the sunshine.

Both the caterpillar and adults feed on the flower heads of red clover

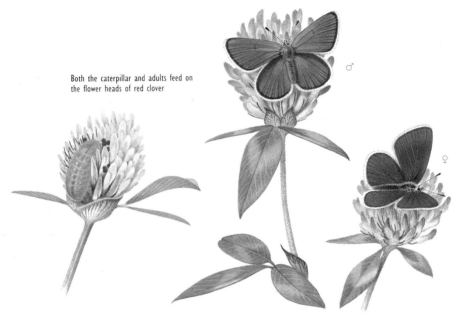

| | |
|---|---|
| J | ✓ |
| F | ✓ |
| M | ✓ |
| A | ✓ |
| M | ✓ ▸ |
| J | · ▸ 🦋 |
| J | · ✓ ▸ 🦋 |
| A | ✓ |
| S | ✓ |
| O | ✓ |
| N | ✓ |
| D | ✓ |

**KEY FEATURES:** The male is deep violet-blue, with obscure dark borders, the female is plain brown with no orange markings, both have clear white fringes. The undersides of the sexes are similar, the female being slightly darker, and the absence of marginal markings and the central band of black spots are diagnostic.

**HABITAT:** Flies in damp, flower-rich hay meadows and hillsides, sometimes on drier scrubby areas, up to 1000m.

**FREQUENCY:** Quite common in central and southern Europe and Fennoscandia but more local in northern France and Belgium where it has suffered from the destruction of unimproved grasslands.

**LIFE HISTORY:** The eggs are laid singly on the flowerheads of red clover and possibly kidney vetch. The young caterpillar starts to feed on the flowers and tender shoots but hibernates in August before fully grown. It continues to feed in early spring and is ready for pupation in May, having been in the larval stage for about ten months. The chrysalis is formed amongst vegetation near the ground and lasts for about two weeks when the butterflies begin to emerge in June. Males usually appear a few days before the females. In most northerly regions there is one generation but further south there may be more.

Little variation to the uppersides but the spots on the underside are sometimes almost absent or may be large and elongated. The base of the hindwings have a blue dusting of scales.

## LOOKALIKES

**Cranberry Blue** *Vacciniina optilete*
Male has an intense violet-blue upperside and clear white wing fringes. Female also has violet-blue basal suffusions to grey-brown wings. Undersides similar in both sexes, with an orange blotch near the margin, containing a blue-centred, black spot. Found in Fenno-scandia and eastern Europe, just reaching south-eastern France. It flies in July and August on acidic bogs, open forest clearings and wet wooded mountain-sides, where *Vaccinium*, the larval foodplants, grow.

**Alpine Blue** *Albulina orbitulus*
Forewings of the male are pointed and bright sky-blue with narrow black margins. The brown female often has a suffusion of blue scales and sometimes a pale blue central spot on her forewings. The undersides are pale greyish-brown with inconspicuous spots on the forewings and with large pale blotches on the hindwings that lack the black centres. Apart from the Alps, it is found only in the damp mountains of central Norway and Sweden. It flies in June and July, often in the company of the Cranberry Blue. Females lay their eggs on alpine milk-vetch.

ssp. *aquilo* ♂

**Glandon Blue** *Agriades glandon*
Occurs in three widely separated European populations, with the tiny sub-species *aquilo* flying on exposed, crumbling mountainsides in northern Fennoscandia. It is a fast flying, inconspicuous butterfly which, because of its restricted distribution and habitat requirements, make it unlikely to be confused with other species.

**Osiris Blue** *Cupido osiris*
Smaller, male with clear, black margins to wings. Underside greyer, with the central band of spots in a straighter line on both wings. It does not occur further north than the French/German border.

# Chalkhill Blue

*Lysandra coridon*

A lovely butterfly of uncultivated calcareous downlands, the distinctive, pale, silvery-blue male contrasting with the comparatively drab female. Both sexes frequent a wide variety of flowers on warm, sunny days, with a preference for knapweeds, scabiouses and other purple flowers.

J
F
M
A
M
J
J
A
S
O
N
D

**KEY FEATURES:** The silvery, blue-green ground colour of the male, bordered by broad black margins on the forewings and with black spots on the hindwings, is diagnostic. The female, however, is more difficult to differentiate from other female Blues, though the Common Blue lacks the chequered wing fringes. The female Adonis Blue has chequered fringes and is very similar but the pale scales around the outer edge of the hindwings' marginal spots are blue, not silver, as in the Chalkhill Blue. The underside of the male's wings are ashy-grey, darker on the hindwing, with black spots broadly ringed with white. The female's underside is similar, though of a darker cinnamon brown.

**HABITAT:** Restricted to calcareous chalk and limestone grasslands and warm flowery downland slopes.

**FREQUENCY:** A local butterfly but may be abundant in good years. It has declined in many places this century due to the 'improvement' of downland sites for agricultural use. Found throughout most of central Europe, with many named sub-species, but absent from Fennoscandia.

**LIFE HISTORY:** Females lay their eggs on or near horseshoe vetch, the only larval foodplant. The young caterpillar emerges in April, having remained within the eggshell throughout the winter, and feeds, mainly at night, for the next ten weeks. When fully grown, it is clear-green, with bright yellow stripes along the back and sides. It is usually found in the company of ants. The dull, ochreous-green chrysalis is formed in a crevice on or below the ground and lasts for about a month. The Chalkhill Blue is single brooded, flying from June until September.

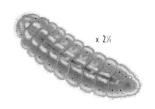

x 2¼

Very variable especially on the underside and much sought after by Victorian butterfly collectors. Female occasionally occurs with the blue uppersides of the male. The caterpillar is a lighter green than that of the Adonis Blue.

## LOOKALIKES

**Damon Blue** *Agrodiaetus damon*
Male bluer, with broader black margins, dark veins radiating inwards and no marginal spots on the hindwings. The female is brown with dusky wing-fringes which lack the conspicuous chequers. Undersides pale, with a distinctive white streak. Found in scattered European populations, including south-eastern Germany, where it flies in grassy meadows and broken woodland, where sainfoin grows. It flies in July and August in a single generation.

**Meleager's Blue** *Meleageria daphnis*
Recognised by the scalloped margin of the hindwings, which is more pronounced in the female, this butterfly is found mainly in the Mediterranean region, eastwards and in an isolated population in central Germany. The underside is pale grey, with black spots heavier on the forewings. It is on the wing from June until August.

**Common Blue** *Polyommatus icarus*
Male distinct violet-blue, the female usually has some blue on the forewings though this may be reduced to a few scales near the body. The wing fringes of both sexes lack any chequering, noticeable on both upper and undersides. (See p.72)

**Adonis Blue** *Lysandra bellargus*
Male distinct, the female is slightly smaller than the Chalkhill Blue, with blue rather than silver scales, on the outer edge of the hindwing spots. The undersides are a more uniform, light, greyish-brown and the white rings surrounding the black spots are less conspicuous. (See p.74)

# Adonis Blue
## Lysandra bellargus

The brilliant electric blue wings of the male Adonis Blue make it a
wonderful site on unimproved downland slopes in high summer.
Like the Chalkhill Blue, the female is mostly brown and both species
can be seen flying together in some places in August and September,
when separation may be difficult.

♀ form *semiceronus*

Adonis Blues on horsehoe vetch
the larval foodplant

♂

♀

x 2¼

| | |
|---|---|
| J | / |
| F | / |
| M | / |
| A | / ♪ |
| M | · ♪ 🦋 |
| J | · / ♪ 🦋 |
| J | · / ♪ |
| A | · / ♪ 🦋 |
| S | · / 🦋 |
| O | · / |
| N | / |
| D | / |

**KEY FEATURES:** The upperside of the male is iridescent sky blue. The underside is grey-
brown and similar to the Common Blue but with chequered fringes to the edges of the
wings. The female has dusky, brown wings, usually with blue scales near the body and
around the outer edge of the hindwings, these are silvery white in the Chalkhill Blue.
Her underside is more ochreous than the male and in both sexes the white rings bordering
the black spots are narrower and more clearly defined than the Chalkhill Blue.
**HABITAT:** Warm flowery, chalk and limestone downs, where the herb-rich turf is short
and exposed to the sun. Further south it is more tolerant of higher vegetation.
**FREQUENCY:** Local and restricted to calcareous soils where horseshoe vetch grows but
some years it can appear in large numbers. It is widespread and commoner throughout
the rest of Europe, but absent from Fennoscandia.
**LIFE HISTORY:** Eggs are laid only on horseshoe vetch in England but in other parts
of Europe, crown vetch may be used. The young caterpillar of the second brood
hibernates while small and resumes feeding the following spring. It is similar to the
Chalkhill Blue but because of the different stages of over-wintering, caterpillars of the
Adonis Blue are fully grown by late April, whereas those of the Chalkhill Blue are still
small. It also differs by being darker green and in feeding by day. Both caterpillar and
chrysalis are tended by ants, the pupal stage lasting about three weeks. Butterflies of
the second generation fly until late September, making it one of the last downland butterflies of the year.

The spots on the undersides of both sexes are variable. The female often has a flush of purple-blue on the upper-surface, form *semiceronus*.

## LOOKALIKES

**Chalkhill Blue** *Lysandra coridon*
Male distinctive, pale silvery-blue. The female is similar to the Adonis Blue but often appears smokier-brown, with silvery scales around the spots near the hindwing margins. Undersides more openly marked with white. Both species often occur together. (See p.70)

**Common Blue** *Polyommatus icarus*
The male is violet-blue, the female brown, often with an extensive blue flush and with well developed orange lunules. The main distinguishing features are the wing fringes which lack the black chequering. It occurs commonly on calcareous downland. (See p.74)

**Turquoise Blue** *Plebicular dorylas*
Male an intense silver-blue. The female resembles other Blues but the undersides of both sexes are diagnostic. Underside spots are sparse near the base and absent from the cell of the forewing, the remaining forewing spots are bolder than those of the hindwing. Wing margins have characteristic white borders, which give the male especially, a pale appearance. It flies from June until August, on dry calcareous soils where kidney vetch, the larval foodplant grows. Found in southern France, Germany and Scandinavia.

**Amanda's Blue** *Agrodiaetus amanda*
One of the largest of the Blue butterflies, the male's upperside is bright, sky-blue, with dark borders and veins that broaden towards the margins. The female is typically brown but further north some specimens may be predominantly blue. The underside is pale, greyish-buff with markings small but clear. There is no spot in the cell of the forewing and the wing-fringes are not chequered. It is a sedate flier, over damp, fertile meadows in eastern Germany and southern Fennoscandia, from May until July.

# Common Blue

*Polyommatus icarus*

The most common and widespread of the Blues and along with the Holly Blue the most frequently encountered. It can be seen in flowery places from sea level to mountainsides, and has a particular liking for the nectar of yellow flowers. At night it roosts communally amongst grasses, head downwards, often in the company of other species of Blue and Argus.

Male Common Blue on bird's foot trefoil

Blue ♀

Females range from all brown to predominantly blue, with specimens in Ireland and Scotland being especially brightly marked. The caterpillar is green with a darker dorsal stripe and is well camouflaged among the leaves of its foodplant.

x 2¼

| | | | |
|---|---|---|---|
| J | / | | |
| F | / | | |
| M | / | | |
| A | / | ♪ | 🦋 |
| M | · | ♪ | 🦋 |
| J | · | / | 🦋 |
| J | · | / ♪ | 🦋 |
| A | · | / ♪ | 🦋 |
| S | · | / ♪ | 🦋 |
| O | · | / ♪ | 🦋 |
| N | / | | |
| D | / | | |

**KEY FEATURES:** The violet-blue upperside of the male, with narrow black margins and clear white fringes is distinctive. Females are variable in the amount of blue on the upperside and they too have white fringes. The underside of the sexes is similar, though the female is browner and slightly bolder, often with well developed orange lunules. A white-ringed black spot is present in the cell of the forewing, this is absent in the similar, Chapman's Blue.

**HABITAT:** Found almost anywhere except barren mountainsides. Particularly abundant on downland, damp flowery hay-meadows and grassy scrubland.

**FREQUENCY:** Common and abundant in many places throughout Europe.

**LIFE HISTORY:** Eggs are laid on a wide range of leguminous plants, particularly, bird's foot trefoil, medicks, rest harrows and clovers. The newly hatched caterpillars feed at first on tender young growth, those that hibernate live for about ten months otherwise, pupation takes place on the ground, after six weeks of growth. In long, hot summers there may be three broods in a year, with butterflies on the wing from April until October.

# LOOKALIKES

Note: Females of several species of Blue can be difficult to separate but the undersides and wing fringes are the best means of identification.

**Adonis Blue** *Lysandra bellargus*
Male brilliant electric blue. The female is dark smokey brown with the fringes clearly chequered on both surfaces, otherwise the undersides are similar to the Common Blue. (See p.72)

♂

♀

**Chalkhill Blue** *Lysandra coridon*
Slightly larger, male chalky blue. The female has dull orange lunules on the smokey brown wings and the scales near the outer margins of the hindwings are white. Wing-fringes with dark chequers. The undersides of both sexes appear chalkier, with more white around the spots. (See p.70)

♂

♂

♀

♂

♀

**Chapman's Blue** *Agrodiaetus thersites*
Both sexes are very similar to the Common Blue but the forewings of the male have pale androconial scales, giving a furry texture. The main means of separation is the underside of the forewing, which lacks the spot in the cell. This is present in the Common Blue. The female upperside ranges from brown to mostly blue. This butterfly occurs on warm flowery slopes and meadows in southern France and Germany southwards and is not found in Britain. The early stages are also like the Common Blue but the caterpillar feeds on sainfoin.

♀

**Brown Argus** *Aricia agestis*
The Brown Argus lacks any trace of blue and the orange markings contrast more clearly with the chocolate brown. On the underside of the forewings, there is no spot in the cell and on the hindwings, the twin spots near the top margin are diagnostic. There is some dark chequering in the wing fringes. (See p.66)

♀

**Silver-studded Blue** *Plebejus argus*
Generally smaller than the Common Blue, the female of this butterfly is smokey brown with varying amounts of blue. The orange lunules are usually duller and further in from the margins. The male has broader black borders to the wings. The underside with its orange band and silver 'studs' is distinctive. (See p.64)

# Duke of Burgundy

*Hamearis lucina*

Sometimes called the 'Duke of Burgundy Fritillary' because of its superficial similarity to some members of that group, this species is unique, in being the only member of the Metalmark (*Riodinidae*) family to occur in Europe, most being found in tropical Central America. It is an attractive lively little butterfly, whose numbers are declining in many places. Males spend much of their time perching conspicuously with wings half open, ready to defend their territories from intruders.

Duke of Burgundies on cowslip, one of the larval foodplants

**KEY FEATURES:** The sexes are similar, though the female is slightly larger and brighter. The hindwings are darker than the forewings and the inner-margins of all wings have a row of inward facing spots. The undersides of the hindwings are distinctive, with two bold rows of cream spots on a red-ochre ground colour.

**HABITAT:** Scrubby chalk downland, open woodland, particularly where coppicing has encouraged plant growth.

**FREQUENCY:** Local in Britain and Fennoscandia becoming commoner further south, though never appearing in large numbers.

**LIFE HISTORY:** The eggs are laid singly or in small batches, usually on the undersides of primrose leaves in wooded areas, and cowslips in more open places. Well developed leaves are chosen for egg laying but the sluggish, brown caterpillars soon reduce them to holey tatters. They live for about six weeks and then leave the foodplants to pupate, secreted on the ground, where they remain for the next ten months. Further south, two generations may appear, but in the north, the short-lived butterfly, is on the wing in from late April until June.

J
F
M
A
M
J
J
A
S
O
N
D

A unique feature of this family are the legs, which are fully functional in the female. In the male however, the forelegs are reduced and not used for walking. The brown hairy caterpillar feeds mainly at night and is easy to find on the underside of leaves.

x 2¼

## LOOKALIKES

**Heath Fritillary** *Mellicta athalia*
This and other *Mellicta* Fritillaries could be confused with the Duke of Burgundy but the uppersides are more evenly chequered and they lack the spots near the edges of the wings. The underside of the hindwings shows less contrast between the banding. (See p.114)

**Small Pearl-bordered Fritillary** *Clossiana selene*
A brighter and more orange looking butterfly, especially in flight. The underside of the hindwings are conspicuously spotted with silver, most noticeable around the wing margins. (See p.108)

**Map Butterfly** *Araschnia levana*
The first brood of this species is of a similar size but it is brighter orange and has a distinctive underside. (See p.96)

**Chequered Skipper** *Carterocephalus palaemon*
The quick flight and orange and black chequers could confuse this butterfly with the Duke of Burgundy but at rest its narrow wings and pale underside make it readily identifiable. (See p.147)

# Monarch

*Danaus plexippus*

A huge migratory butterfly that is only rarely encountered in south-western Britain. Best known for its incredible migrations from North America and Canada, when millions fly south to hibernate communally in the conifer forests of Mexico and California. It is when these migrations occur in the Autumn that some individuals are blown off course across the Atlantic Ocean and arrive on our shores.

Garden plants like buddleia attract
visiting Monarchs in late summer

J
F
M
A
M
J
J
A
S
O
N
D

**KEY FEATURES:** The large size and deep, orange and black colour are sufficient to differentiate this butterfly from all other European species. Even from a distance its strong flapping and gliding flight is characteristic. The sexes are alike but the male has a distinctive black patch of scent scales on vein 2 of the hindwings.

**HABITAT:** A wanderer when it arrives in Britain, most often occurring in gardens and cultivated places where it feeds on autumnal flowers like buddleia and michaelmas daisy.

**FREQUENCY:** First recorded in Britain about 120 years ago, with only about a hundred specimens seen up until the second world war. Since then it has been recorded much more frequently, due mainly to the observations of ornithologists who visit the Scilly Isles in large numbers every Autumn, to record migratory birds from across the Atlantic. The year of greatest abundance was 1981 when more than 130 were recorded.

**LIFE HISTORY:** Having crossed the Atlantic, no Monarch is likely to breed here, as the milkweed, its larval foodplant, is not indigenous. However it can be bred quite easily in captivity and it is likely that some records of this butterfly are of escapees. The eggs are laid singly and hatch within a week. The caterpillar is a voracious eater and is fully grown in just over two weeks. Its bright markings indicate to predators that it contains poisons, obtained from the milkweed, these are passed to the butterfly, making both distasteful. The chrysalis is pale blue-green adorned with a beautiful band and spots of gold spangles, it lasts for about two weeks.

♂

♀

Females lack the sex-brand on the
hindwings and are more heavily
marked with black along the
veins. The fast growing caterpillar
feeds conspicuously on milkweed,
protected by the disagreeable
poisons taken up from the plant.

## LOOKALIKES
No other butterfly in northern Europe could
be mistaken for the Monarch.

# Purple Emperor

*Apatura iris*

**M**agnificent but elusive, the Purple Emperor is a butterfly of mature deciduous woodlands, where males soar above the canopy descending occasionally to feed from damp puddles, excrement and decomposing corpses in forest glades. Females are larger but lack the defracted purple sheen that glances from the males' wings. Though widespread throughout Europe, it is threatened in some places by the fragmentation of ancient forests.

x 1½

♂

| | |
|---|---|
| J | ✓ |
| F | ✓ |
| M | ✓ |
| A | ✓ |
| M | ✓ |
| J | ✓ ♪ 🦋 |
| J | · ♪ 🦋 |
| A | · ✓ 🦋 |
| S | · ✓ |
| O | ✓ |
| N | ✓ |
| D | ✓ |

**KEY FEATURES:** Both sexes are deep brown-black with contrasting white bands and spots but it is only the male who has the gleaming purple sheen which catches the light at certain angles. The forewing has an obscure black blotch towards the outer margin, which, in the Lesser Purple Emperor, is clearly out-lined in orange. The other feature distinguishing it from this species, is the spur, projecting from the outer margin of the white band, on the hindwing. The underside of the hindwing is brighter and shows more contrast.

**HABITAT:** Deciduous woodland glades and forest edges, where large oaks and sallows grow.

**FREQUENCY:** Found throughout central Europe eastward and including southern Britain and Denmark. Restricted to mature woodland, where, although present in fair numbers, it may often be overlooked, as it spends much time high in the treetops.

**LIFE HISTORY:** The eggs are laid singly on the upperside of sallow leaves growing in sheltered woodland edges. The young caterpillar, which resembles a small brown slug, hibernates near a leaf bud and resumes feeding in the spring, when it turns an attractive granular, greenish-blue. It is perfectly camouflaged amongst sallow leaves, where it pupates after more than ten months as a caterpillar. The elegant leaf-green chrysalis is suspended from the underside of a leaf, where it stays for two weeks before hatching in late June or early July (see p.15). The Purple Emperor is single brooded, butterflies appear until the end of August.

Variation is unusual but very rarely specimens occur with little or no white on the upperside. This is known as aberration *iole* and was highly prized by Victorian collectors.

## LOOKALIKES

♀

♂

♂

♀

**Lesser Purple Emperor** *Apatura ilia*
Very like the Purple Emperor but rather smaller, this species has a similar distribution but does not occur so far to the north west, being absent from Britain and Fennoscandia. The main distinguishing features are the orange-ringed black spot on the upperside of the forewings and the white band on the hindwings, which lacks the spur on the outer edge. The underside of the hindwing is also duller. It sometimes appears in a beautiful orange form *clytie*. Flies in similar habitats to the Purple Emperor but prefers slightly damper woodlands. The early stages are also similar but there is a preference for aspen as the larval foodplant. Occurs either in one or two broods from May until September.

**NOTE:**
**Poplar Admiral** *Limenitis populi*
A grand butterfly, even larger than the Purple Emperor. Both sexes have conspicuous orange lunules on the hindwings, with no trace of the iridescent sheen of the male Purple Emperor. Flies in damp deciduous woodland where aspen grows. (See p.84)

# White Admiral

*Limenitis camilla*

A butterfly of open woodland glades, where its effortless, gliding flight through dappled sunlight in search of bramble flowers, is unique in northern forests. Unlike many woodland species it has enjoyed an increase in its distribution in recent decades, due mainly to changes in woodland management. This has resulted in more areas becoming overgrown and partially shaded, much to the liking of this butterfly.

Adult on bramble

x 1½

| | | |
|---|---|---|
| J | / | |
| F | / | |
| M | / | |
| A | / | |
| M | / ▸ | |
| J | / ▸ | ✹ |
| J · | / ▸ | ✹ |
| A · | / | ✹ |
| S | / | |
| O | / | |
| N | / | |
| D | / | |

**KEY FEATURES:** This medium sized chocolate-brown and white butterfly, is much smaller than the Poplar Admiral or the Purple Emperor, which may share the same habitats. Its preference for visiting flowers also distinguishes it from these two butterflies who spend most of their lives high in the forest canopy. The lovely underside with the broad white bands, lacks the bluish-green margins of the Poplar Admiral.

**HABITAT:** Open woodland glades with dappled sunlight breaking through, often amongst mixed conifer and deciduous plantations.

**FREQUENCY:** Restricted to woodlands, it may however be quite common in some years and is expanding its range in Britain.

**LIFE HISTORY:** The strange spiny egg is laid on straggly growths of honeysuckle growing in partial shade (see p.11). The young caterpillar is easy to find, as it feeds on the outer edges of the leaf-tip, either side of the midrib on which it rests. It adds to its camouflage by adorning itself and the midrib, with its own droppings. Whilst still small it constructs a shelter, called a hibernaculum, made from part of a leaf and here it remains until spring. It resumes feeding after seven months in hibernation and when fully grown the attractive pale-green caterpillar is much harder to find than when it was small. The horned chrysalis is green and brown and adorned with beautiful silver spots, hangs suspended below a leaf stem for about two weeks. The first butterflies are on the wing in late June and fly in a single brood until August.

The sexes are similar, with some variation in the amount of white on the upperside. This, in the extreme form *nigrina,* may be completely absent. The caterpillar rests with only the central pairs of legs in contact with the stem.

## Lookalikes

**Map Butterfly** *Araschnia levana*
The second brood of this butterfly resembles the White Admiral but it is much smaller. (See p.96)

**Southern White Admiral** *Limenitis reducta*
Superficially similar to the White Admiral but distinguished by the clear white spot in the cell of the forewings and the more broken white band on the hindwings. There is a row of pale blue spots near the edge of the wings, which have a steely-blue sheen at certain angles. The underside of the hindwings has a broad pale-blue base and there is only one row of black spots towards the margin, whereas the White Admiral has two rows. It flies from July until August in scrubby woodland where honeysuckle, its caterpillar's foodplant, grows. Distributed mainly in central southern Europe including southern Germany and France but also occurs in an isolated population in north-western France.

**Purple Emperor** *Apatura iris*
Often found in the same localities as the White Admiral, this is a bigger butterfly, with the male having a deep purple sheen. The underside is diagnostic. (See p.80)

**Poplar Admiral** *Limenitis populi*
A much larger butterfly with conspicuous orange lunules on the upperside and bluish-green borders on the underside of the wings. It flies in deciduous woodland where aspens grow, and is more often seen high in the canopy. Absent from Britain, it has a more easterly European distribution. (See p.84)

# Poplar Admiral

*Limenitis populi*

This butterfly is one of the largest of the European Nymphalids. It usually flies high in the canopy of mixed woodlands but occasionally descends to drink from muddy puddles, decaying animal corpses or dung. It has a powerful, gliding flight and its bluish-black and white markings, make it a spectacular sight as it patrols along woodland rides.

Male Poplar Admiral at rest on aspen leaves, the larval foodplant

| | |
|---|---|
| J | ✦ |
| F | ✦ |
| M | ✦ |
| A | ✦ |
| M | ✦ ✦ |
| J | • ✦ |
| J | • ✦ |
| A | • ✦ |
| S | ✦ |
| O | ✦ |
| N | ✦ |
| D | ✦ |

**KEY FEATURES:** The hindwings have a broad white central band, with more broken spots on the forewings, including a central spot which is absent in all but the Southern White Admiral. The borders of the wings have a blue-green sheen with characteristic orange lunules on the inside. The underside of the wings have bluish borders with double black lines.

**HABITAT:** Damp woodland margins and paths where aspens grow in sheltered sunny rides.

**FREQUENCY:** A generally local butterfly, absent from Britain but in good years may be quite common in southern Sweden.

**LIFE HISTORY:** The egg is like that of the White Admiral but is laid on aspen, or more rarely on other poplars. When young, the caterpillar resembles a bird dropping, feeding at the leaf-tip either side of the mid-rib on which it rests. In the Autumn it makes a tubular structure, a hibernaculum, from a fragment of leaf, which it attaches to a twig. It remains hidden within this tube throughout the winter and resumes feeding in the spring. Gradually it turns from brown and white, to green and brown, with two knobbly horns near its head. The attractive chrysalis is suspended from a silken pad on an aspen leaf. The flight period lasts from mid-June until the end of July. Because of this short flight period, bad weather sometimes affects the success of the butterfly the following year.

The white markings are variable,
sometimes being almost absent,
when it is known as form *tremulae*.

♀

## LOOKALIKES

♀

**Purple Emperor** *Apatura iris*
The male has a distinctive purple sheen at certain
angles, the female is similar but lacks the orange
lunules and the white spot in the cell of the forewings.
(See p.80)

♀

**White Admiral** *Limenitis camilla*
Smaller and without the white spot in cell of forewings,
or orange lunules. Underside of hindwings lacks the
bluish-green borders. (See p.82)

♂

**Southern White Admiral** *Limenitis reducta*
Has a clear white spot in the cell of the forewing but is
much smaller than the Poplar Admiral. Wings lack
orange lunules and have a row of pale blue spots and a
steely blue sheen at certain angles. Underside of hindwings has a plain, pale blue base and no blue and black
bands to the margin. (See p.83)

# Large Tortoiseshell

*Nymphalis polychloros*

A fast flying rarity in northern Europe, this fine insect, closely related to the Camberwell Beauty, shares its liking for sap exuding from tree wounds and is less often seen feeding from flowers, like the Small Tortoiseshell. It is shy and difficult to catch or photograph, disappearing quickly into the treetops when alarmed. Notoriously erratic in its appearance, some years it is entirely absent from places where it was previously quite common.

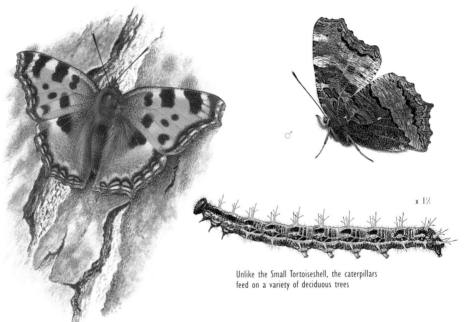

♂

x 1½

Unlike the Small Tortoiseshell, the caterpillars feed on a variety of deciduous trees

| J | ♠ |
| F | ♠ |
| M | ♠ |
| A | ♠ |
| M | ♠ |
| J | ♪ |
| J | ♪ ♠ |
| A | ♠ |
| S | ♠ |
| O | ♠ |
| N | ♠ |
| D | ♠ |

**KEY FEATURES:** Differs from the Small Tortoiseshell, with which it sometimes hibernates, by the absence of white towards the tip of the forewings and the yellowish-brown ground colour which is apparent in flight. The underside has less contrast, particularly on the forewings.

**HABITAT:** Sheltered woodland clearings and sunny glades where elms and willows grow. Further south it occurs in gardens and orchards.

**FREQUENCY:** Virtually extinct in southern Britain and very rare in Fennoscandia, becoming more frequent further south. Reasons for its fluctuation in numbers are unclear but likely to include an intolerance to climatic changes and vulnerability to parasitism.

**LIFE HISTORY:** The eggs are laid in bands around the twigs of elm, and less often on willow, poplar and cherry. They hatch after three weeks and the caterpillars live communally on conspicuous webs. When mature they drop to the ground and crawl some distance from the foodplant to pupate. The chrysalis lasts for two weeks and the first butterflies begin to emerge in July. It is single brooded and not long after their emergence adults enter into hibernation in hollow trees, wood stacks or sheds. They appear again the following March along with other hibernating butterflies.

Sexes are similar with very little variation amongst adults.

## LOOKALIKES

**Small Tortoiseshell** *Aglais urticae*
Brighter orange ground colour and with a white spot near the tip of the forewings. The undersides have more contrast, the forewing being very pale. Very common. (See p.94)

**False Comma** *Nymphalis vau-album*
The four conspicuous white spots on the heavily marked upperside are diagnostic. The underside is beautifully marbled though variable with a small white 'C' in the centre. Rarer, with an even more easterly distribution than the Yellow-legged Tortoiseshell, a few specimens have been recorded in south-eastern Fennoscandia.

**Yellow-legged Tortoiseshell**
*Nymphalis xanthomelas*
Clear, deep-orange wings, dark borders wider, with suffused edges. The underside is very similar but the legs are yellowish-brown. Very rare, only occasional in southern Fennoscandia and eastern Germany. It flies from July to September in a single generation.

# Peacock
*Inachis io*

No other butterfly resembles the Peacock, which is still, fortunately, a familiar sight in high summer to anyone with a flower garden. Buddleia and michaelmas daisies are great favourites but further into the countryside they regularly visit thistles, knapweeds, scabiouses and many other wild flowers. It is one of the earliest butterflies to emerge from hibernation in the spring, when males defend their territories from other males or bask in the warm sunshine.

Peacocks are often seen around nettle patches, the only larval foodplant

| J |  |
|---|---|
| F |  |
| M |  |
| A |  |
| M |  |
| J |  |
| J |  |
| A |  |
| S |  |
| O |  |
| N |  |
| D |  |

**KEY FEATURES:** Unmistakable on the upperside. However, the underside may cause some confusion, particularly when it is hibernating or when resting with the forewings obscured by the hindwings. The Peacock is the darkest of all the Vanessids that hibernate as adults.

**HABITAT:** Almost anywhere, including open woodland glades, chalk downland, damp meadows and gardens, wherever there is an abundance of nettles.

**FREQUENCY:** Widespread and common throughout central Europe but rare in northern Scotland and Fennoscandia. Numbers fluctuate from year to year and in good years dozens can be seen feeding from flowers, along woodland rides and on downland.

**LIFE HISTORY:** The green eggs are laid in large batches on the underside of young nettle leaves in May (see p.11). They hatch after two weeks and the caterpillars live gregariously in conspicuous clusters on webs spun over the leaves. When fully grown after about four weeks, they disperse from the foodplant and seek a sheltered sight to pupate. The chrysalis may be green or brown depending on its surroundings, and it remains, suspended from a silken pad, for two weeks. After emerging the adults seek out flowers to build up their body reserves ready for hibernation in September. This takes place in hollow trees, woodpiles and sheds, with several sometimes gathering together with Small Tortoiseshells. They emerge in the first warm days of spring, with butterflies that hatched in August, sometimes surviving until the following June.

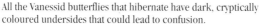

x 1½

When the wings are suddenly flashed open, the spectacular eye-spots may alarm potential predators. This action is sometimes accompanied by a hissing, made by rubbing the wings together. The caterpillar is longer than the Small Tortoiseshell, and is black and covered in white speckles.

LOOKALIKES   All the Vanessid butterflies that hibernate have dark, cryptically coloured undersides that could lead to confusion.

**Small Tortoiseshell**
*Aglais urticae* (See p.94)

**Comma**
*Polygonia c-album* (See p.93)

**Red Admiral**
*Vanessa atalanta* (See p.90)

**Camberwell Beauty** *Nymphalis antiopa*
Also known as the 'Mourning Cloak' and 'White Bordered' the present English name for this butterfly comes from Camberwell, the locality in London where it was first discovered, about two hundred and fifty years ago. The ochreous yellow borders to the wings, which fade to white after hibernation, make it easy to identify, as it is unlike any other European butterfly. It is nomadic and occurs in a variety of open habitats including gardens, especially where there is an abundance of willow. The eggs are laid in bands of 50–150 around the twigs of various willows or occasionally on poplar or birch. The caterpillars are gregarious and feed in conspicuous groups until they are ready to pupate, often well away from the foodplant (see p.14). Adults emerge in late summer and it is from August to October that most migrants reach Britain, mainly from Scandinavia. Widely distributed throughout central and north eastern Europe, being particularly common in central Sweden but rare in Britain.

# Red Admiral
## *Vanessa atalanta*

This beautiful butterfly which migrates to northern Europe each spring, is a familiar sight in parks and gardens. It prefers purple and pink flowers as well as the sweet juice from rotting fruit and sap. In late autumn it is a frequent visitor to ivy flowers, where it jostles for nectar in the company of wasps and other insects. Occasionally, on warm evenings, it flies at dusk. Rarely capable of surviving northern winters however, in recent years there have been more frequent reports of specimens being seen in early spring, suggesting successful over-wintering.

Sedum is often a favoured nectar source in late summer

| | | | |
|---|---|---|---|
| J | | | |
| F | | | |
| M | | | |
| A | · | ╱ | ₩ |
| M | · | ╱ | ₩ |
| J | · | ╱ ╲ | ₩ |
| J | · | ╱ ╲ | ₩ |
| A | · | ╱ ╲ | ₩ |
| S | · | ╱ ╲ | ₩ |
| O | | ╱ ╲ | ₩ |
| N | | ╱ ╲ | ₩ |
| D | | | |

**KEY FEATURES:** The striking black, red and white is unmistakable, with only the Indian Red Admiral of the Canary Islands showing any resemblance. At rest, with forewings lowered, there could be some confusion with other common Vanessids but the pale blotch on the top edge of the hindwings is diagnostic.

**HABITAT:** Found almost anywhere, particularly gardens, old orchards and uncultivated land where there is an abundance of flowers, nettles and rotting fruit.

**FREQUENCY:** A common butterfly, widespread throughout Europe but in the north its numbers fluctuate depending on migration.

**LIFE HISTORY:** The egg is laid singly on the upperside edge of a tender nettle leaf, or more rarely, on pellitory-of-the-wall. After a week the young caterpillar emerges and after eating its eggshell spins a tent at the base of the leaf. As it eats and grows it constructs larger tents made up from several leaves, it remains hidden in these until full grown. Its colour varies from pale greyish-yellow to predominantly black with yellow spots, adorned with short yellow spines. It lives for about three weeks and the chrysalis is formed suspended from the roof of the tent. Only one generation is produced a year but egg laying can extend from April until September. Butterflies that emerge in the north undertake a partial re-migration but many expire on the way.

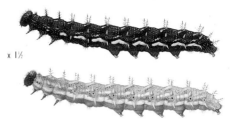

x 1½

There is rarely any variation in the markings and the sexes are similar. The caterpillar is easy to find within its conspicuous leafy shelter.

## LOOKALIKES

The undersides of several of the other common Vanessids could be confused with the Red Admiral. All four species sometimes feed together on the same plants.

**Small Tortoiseshell**
*Aglais urticae*
Plainer, with a distinctly paler outer half to the hindwings and no red or white on the forewings. (See p.94)

**Peacock** *Inachis io*
Uniform brownish-black with a slatey-blue sheen to the hindwings. (See p.88)

**Scarlet Tiger Moth** *Callimorpha dominula*
To the butterfly watcher, unfamiliar with moths, this day-flying species could cause some confusion. It shares the same colour combinations as the Red Admiral and can be seen flying purposefully in warm summer sunshine. Normally it appears locally in water meadows, along river banks, fens and coastal gullies, but in some years, the most recent being the early 1990s, populations increase enormously and individuals disperse and form colonies almost anywhere, including towns and gardens. The attractive yellow and black, hairy caterpillar feeds from autumn until spring on a wide range of plants, including comfrey, hemp agrimony, garden mint, stinging nettles and docks.

**Painted Lady** *Vanessa cardui*
Paler, with intricately marked hindwings and a rosy flush to the forewings. (See p.92)

# Painted Lady

*Vanessa cardui*

Almost cosmopolitan, the Painted Lady is more widely distributed than any other butterfly, and along with the Monarch is one of the best known migrants. It is continuously brooded and has no hibernating stage, which means it is resident only in warm climates, butterflies that appear in Europe being migrants from North Africa. Some years the population erupts and vast numbers disperse from their breeding grounds. The most recent of these was in 1996 when tens of millions swarmed into Britain and could be seen virtually everywhere.

x 1½

Painted Lady on mallow

| | | | |
|---|---|---|---|
| J | | | |
| F | | | |
| M | | | |
| A | • | / | 🦋 |
| M | • | / | 🦋 |
| J | • | / ♪ | 🦋 |
| J | • | / ♪ | 🦋 |
| A | • | / ♪ | 🦋 |
| S | • | / ♪ | 🦋 |
| O | • | / ♪ | 🦋 |
| N | | | |
| D | | | |

**KEY FEATURES:** It is unlikely that this butterfly could be mistaken for any other northern European butterfly, the underside in particular being unique. The exceedingly rare American Painted Lady is unlikely to be encountered.

**HABITAT:** In good years it is ubiquitous, occurring wherever flowers, particularly thistles, grow.

**FREQUENCY:** Unpredictable in its appearances, sometimes almost absent, followed by periods of abundance.

**LIFE HISTORY:** The egg is laid singly on a wide range of plants, including, thistles, nettles and mallows. As the young caterpillar grows it constructs a tent from the leaves of the foodplant, similar to the Red Admiral. It remains living concealed until nearly full grown and then emerges to complete its growth in a more exposed position. The elegant chrysalis is variable in colour, often smokey-grey washed with gold. It is suspended from a stem inside its leafy shelter and the adult emerges after two weeks.

Note: The caterpillar is slimmer than the Red Admiral and the yellow dashes along the sides are narrower and more continuous.

# Comma

*Polygonia c-album*

The ragged torn outline and the white 'C' on its underside, make the Comma easily identified. Remarkably well camouflaged when roosting or hibernating, it is virtually impossible to detect amongst withered brown leaves. This is in marked contrast to the rich orange upperside, as the Comma dashes and glides, Fritillary-like, along woodland glades. It has a liking for bramble flowers and fermenting fruit and when it is not feeding, spends much of its time basking in the sun. In Britain, it is fortunate that this once very rare butterfly has increased its range and is now quite common in southern England and Wales.

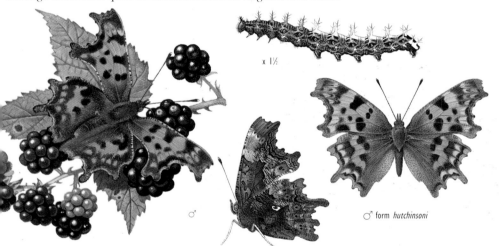

x 1½

♂

♂ form *hutchinsoni*

**KEY FEATURES:** In flight it could be mistaken for some of the medium-sized Fritillaries but the ragged outline is unique, with only the Southern Comma of the eastern Mediterranean being at all similar. The underside of the female is plainer and the wings are less deeply scalloped than the male. Form *hutchinsoni* is lighter on both surfaces.

**HABITAT:** Open woodland rides, hedgerows, gardens and old orchards.

**FREQUENCY:** Common throughout Europe but absent from the extreme north.

**LIFE HISTORY:** Eggs are laid singly, usually on stinging nettle and less often on hop, currants, elms and sallows. Though it is said to mimic a bird dropping, the caterpillar is lovely, with a distinctive, white, spiny saddle. It rests, curled on either leaf surface and does not form a protective tent from leaves, unlike its near relatives. The cryptically marked chrysalis is reddish-brown with several gleaming silver spots, it is suspended low amongst the vegetation and lasts for about two weeks. The butterflies appear in two generations a year, making the Comma unique amongst the hibernators, though in Fennoscandia it may be single brooded in poor years. A proportion of the Commas produced by the spring caterpillars are brighter ochreous-orange and are called form *hutchinsoni*. These, unlike their typically marked relatives, mate and lay eggs, producing normal adults later in the year. Both generations then enter hibernation amongst leaves at the base of tree trunks.

| Month | Egg | Larva | Pupa | Adult |
|-------|-----|-------|------|-------|
| J |  |  |  | ▲ |
| F |  |  |  | ▲ |
| M |  |  |  | ▼ |
| A | • | ∕ |  | ▼ |
| M | • | ∕ |  | ▼ |
| J |  | ∕ | ♪ | ▼ |
| J | • | ∕ | ♪ | ▼ |
| A | • | ∕ | ♪ | ▼ |
| S |  |  | ♪ | ▼ |
| O |  |  |  | ▼ |
| N |  |  |  | ▲ |
| D |  |  |  | ▲ |

# Small Tortoiseshell

*Aglais urticae*

Perhaps the most familiar of European butterflies, the name Small Tortoiseshell is still often confused with that of its relative, the Red Admiral. A strong flyer which can be seen on warm spring days after hibernation, as well as in late autumn, when it is a frequent visitor to gardens, with a particular liking for the flowers of buddleia, sedum and michaelmas daisy. One of the longest lived butterflies, some individuals that survive the winter may live for up to eleven months.

The Small Tortoiseshell is a regular visitor to garden buddleias

Hibernating adult

| J | |
|---|---|
| F | |
| M | |
| A | |
| M | |
| J | |
| J | |
| A | |
| S | |
| O | |
| N | |
| D | |

**KEY FEATURES:** Sexes are similar and the distinctive markings of the upperside make it unlikely to be confused with other common Vanessids. The white mark towards the tip of the wings distinguishes it from the Large Tortoiseshell, which is much rarer. When at rest, with forewings lowered and obscured by the hindwings, careful examination is necessary. Flight is direct, interspersed with glides, though males often spiral high into the sky with other males, competing for territory.

**HABITAT:** Found throughout the region in any flowery areas where nettles occur. Common in gardens and urban areas, specimens are often found hibernating in houses and sheds.

**FREQUENCY:** Often very common, occurring in two generations lasting from March to November. In northern areas only one generation appears.

**LIFE-HISTORY:** The female lays her egg batch on the underside of nettle leaves, usually choosing young plants growing in sunny sheltered positions. The caterpillars form a silken tent and live gregariously until almost fully grown, when they disperse to other nearby nettles. The chrysalis, which may be golden-green or brown, is suspended either on the food-plant or more often under ledges or walls (see p.15).

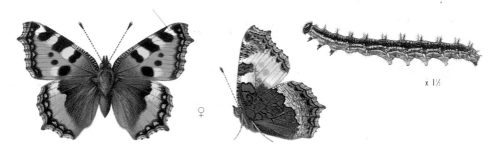

x 1½

Markings vary slightly between individuals but extreme aberrations are rare. Specimens from cooler regions often appear darker. The yellow and black spiny caterpillar may sometimes occur in a brighter yellow form. Caterpillars of the Peacock are similarly gregarious but are velvet black with white speckles.

## LOOKALIKES

**Large Tortoiseshell**  *Nymphalis polychloros*
Ground colour less brilliant giving a yellowish-brown appearance in flight. The wing-tips lack the white patches. Underside, particularly the forewing, shows less contrast. (See p.86)

**Peacock**  *Inachis io*
Upperside quite distinctive but the underside is darker than the Small Tortoiseshell, with a bluish sheen. Both species often hibernate together in out buildings. (See p.88)

**Red Admiral**  *Vanessa atalanta*
Found in similar habitats. Underside of hindwings differ in having a pale yellow blotch and attractive, variegated marbling. (See p.90)

*95*

# Map Butterfly
## *Araschnia levana*

Alively little butterfly of open woodland glades, best known for the remarkable difference between its spring and summer generations. The common name comes from the beautifully intricate underside, which is unlike any other European butterfly. Absent from Britain, it was however, introduced about eighty five years ago and again in the early 1990s, causing great excitement and then annoyance. The first introduction was exterminated by a disapproving collector, the second remains and is reinforced each year with stock from various continental populations.

Creeping thistle is a favourite nectar source for butterflies of the 2nd brood

♂

2nd brood ♂

♀

| | | |
|---|---|---|
| J | ➤ | |
| F | ➤ | |
| M | ➤ | |
| A | ➤ | |
| M | · ➤ | 🦋 |
| J | · ✒ ➤ | 🦋 |
| J | · ✒ ➤ | 🦋 |
| A | · ✒ ➤ | 🦋 |
| S | ✒ ➤ | |
| O | ➤ | |
| N | ➤ | |
| D | ➤ | |

**KEY FEATURES:** The markings of the first brood are Fritillary like but there are white spots near the wing tips and small blue lunules around the edge of the hindwings. The second brood resembles a small White Admiral but has orange lines and markings towards the edges of the wings. The abdomens of both generations are clearly lined with white between each segment.

**HABITAT:** Forest clearings and damp sheltered scrubby places, with an abundance of nettles.

**FREQUENCY:** Common throughout central and eastern Europe, populations in its northern range have expanded in recent decades. Increasing, though still uncommon in southern Fennoscandia, absent from Britain apart from introductions.

**LIFE HISTORY:** Eggs are laid in columns hanging from the underside of nettle leaves and resemble strings of flowers, unlike the eggs of any other nettle feeder. The caterpillars are gregarious until their final instar, when they disperse to surrounding plants. They resemble Small Tortoiseshells being mainly black with rusty markings along the sides and covered in pale speckles, however the distinguishing feature is the head, which has two prominent spines. The stout spiny chrysalis is various shades of brown, with silver spots and is attached to dried vegetation. Chrysalises from the second generation of butterflies hibernate, with the first adults appearing the following May. The second generation flies in July and August and in hot summers a third brood may occur.

1st brood

♀

Females tend to be larger with broader wings, otherwise, the sexes are similar. The caterpillar is like the Small Tortoiseshell but has two prominent head spines.

x 1½

## LOOKALIKES

♂

**Small Pearl-bordered Fritillary** *Clossiana selene*
Some of the small, early flying Fritillaries could be mistaken for the Map but their spotting tends to be more regular and their undersides are less confusingly marked, often adorned with silver 'pearls'. (See p.108)

♀

**Duke of Burgundy** *Hamaeris lucina*
Smaller and darker, particularly the hindwings and with a row of small black spots around the edges of the wings. (See p.76)

♂

**White Admiral** *Limenitis camilla*
Upperside markings very like the 2nd brood Map but much larger and with no orange around the borders. (See p.82)

# Silver-washed Fritillary

*Argynnis paphia*

The largest and most spectacular of the British Fritillaries and in the rest of Europe surpassed in size only by the Cardinal. The male has a powerful gliding flight and in hot summers, many can be seen jostling for nectar on bramble patches, a sight less frequent now in southern Britain. It is a sun lover and in dull weather and at night butterflies seek shelter in trees. The female is less often seen but does descend from the tree tops to visit flowers and to be courted in open glades by males.

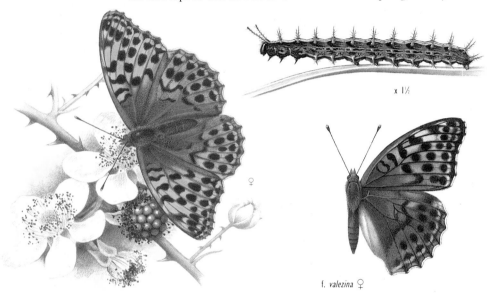

x 1½

♀

f. *valezina* ♀

| | |
|---|---|
| J | / |
| F | / |
| M | / |
| A | / |
| M | / ♪ |
| J | / ♪ ✖ |
| J | · ♪ ✖ |
| A | · / ✖ |
| S | · / ✖ |
| O | / |
| N | / |
| D | / |

**KEY FEATURES:** The male's upperside is rich orange, strongly spotted, and with four broad sex-brands along the veins of the forewings. Both sexes have pointed forewings with a concave outer-edge. The female is usually larger and the wings more ochreous in colour, suffused with olive-green at the bases and on the hindwings. She also occurs with a dramatic bluish-green wash, known as form *valezina*. The underside of the hindwings is bronze-green, with a pinkish tinge and washed with four bands of silver.

**HABITAT:** Sunny woodland rides with an abundance of brambles, over-grown country lanes and hedgerows.

**FREQUENCY:** Common throughout in the south but absent from northern Fennoscandia. In Britain it has declined but remains locally common in the South West, Wales and Ireland.

**LIFE HISTORY:** The egg is laid in a crevice at the base of a tree trunk which has dog violets growing nearby. After emerging, the tiny caterpillar eats its eggshell then immediately enters into hibernation, in a nook in the bark. The following spring it descends to search for violets where it feeds until June. The full grown caterpillar is active in sunshine but it also spends much of its time basking on dry vegetation where it is difficult to spot. After ten months as a caterpillar it pupates suspended amongst vegetation by a silken pad (see p.15). The chrysalis stage lasts for two to three weeks, with butterflies appearing from June to September in a single generation.

The male is rich orange, with conspicuous sex-brands on the forewings. The caterpillar has a conspicuous double cream stripe down its back.

## LOOKALIKES

**Cardinal** *Argynnis pandora*
The largest of the Fritillaries, the Pandora is mainly a southern and eastern European species but does occur locally along the western coast of France. Both sexes are darker and more heavily suffused with green on the upperside. The characteristic rose red flush on the underside of the forewings is diagnostic, and the hind-wings are clear blue-green with varying amounts of silver. It occurs in similar habitats to the Silver-washed Fritillary and its caterpillars also feed on violets.
Note: The three other large European Fritillaries that may fly in similar habitats, are; the Dark Green Fritillary (see p.100), High Brown Fritillary (see p.102) and Niobe Fritillary (see p.103).

99

# Dark Green Fritillary

*Argynnis aglaja*

This is the commonest and most widespread of the large Fritillaries. It occurs in a wide range of habitats and its strong determined flight is an asset on wind-swept dunes and cliff tops where it seems at its most numerous. Like all Fritillaries it is a sun lover and is particularly keen on visiting thistles and other purple flowers, although, on coastal dunes, wild privet is a favourite nectar source. Occasionally individuals stray from their usual habitats and turn up in the most unexpected places.

Male Dark Green Fritillary
feeding on wild privet

| | |
|---|---|
| J | ✏ |
| F | ✏ |
| M | ✏ |
| A | ✏ |
| M | ✏ ➤ |
| J | ➤ 🦋 |
| J | · ✏ ➤ 🦋 |
| A | · ✏ 🦋 |
| S | · ✏ 🦋 |
| O | ✏ |
| N | ✏ |
| D | ✏ |

**KEY FEATURES:** The male is fulvous-orange, strongly marked with black and on the forewings, veins 1–4 are slightly thickened with sex-brands. The female is more ochreous with paler creamy spots near the tip of the forewings. In both sexes the crescent-shaped, submarginal spots are bolder than in the High Brown Fritillary and the forewings are more rounded. The underside of the hindwings are predominantly green with no red and the fine trace of silver at the tip of the forewings is nearer to the margin.

**HABITAT:** Chalk and limestone hills, moorlands, dunes and open woodlands with an abundance of wild flowers.

**FREQUENCY:** Found widely throughout Europe, fairly common but affected by the destruction of unimproved meadows.

**LIFE HISTORY:** The eggs are laid near to lush growths of violets, growing in sheltered places. The newly hatched caterpillar hibernates soon after emerging and remains dormant until the following spring. It feeds from April until May and is particularly active in sunshine. The stout curved chrysalis, looks unlike any of the other Fritillaries. Formed inside a loosely constructed shelter of leaves, low down amongst the vegetation, it lasts for about a month and the first adults appear in mid-June. Only one generation occurs, lasting into September.

x 1½

The size of the black spots varies, females, especially in some Scottish populations, being very boldly marked. The restless, black and red caterpillar can sometimes be seen moving rapidly between patches of violets in warm sunshine.

## LOOKALIKES

**High Brown Fritillary** *Argynnis adippe*
The most constant means of identification on the upper-side, is the straight or slightly concave outer edge to the forewings. On the underside of the hindwings, the row of rusty spots with silver centres is diagnostic. (See p.102)

**Pallas's Fritillary** *Argynnis laodice*
This rare Fritillary occasionally migrates into the extreme east of the region where it can be overlooked. Its flight is slow but resembles the Silver-washed Fritillary. However the underside of the hindwing is distinctive, being clearly divided by a ragged, silver-blue line. Flies in July and early August.

# High Brown Fritillary

*Argynnis adippe*

A much scarcer butterfly in the north than the Dark Green Fritillary, this species has declined drastically in Britain over the past 40 years but is still quite common in central and southern Europe. The male has a powerful determined flight and visits the flowers of thistles and bramble. In poor weather, and at night, adults shelter in trees.

x 1½

The caterpillar may appear much darker than the typical form shown here

J ·
F ·
M ·
A ·
M ·
J ·
J ·
A ·
S ·
O ·
N ·
D ·

**KEY FEATURES:** The male is deep fulvous-orange, spotted with black and with prominent sex-brands along veins 2 and 3 of the forewings. The ground colour of the female is unicolorous and unlike the Dark Green Fritillary, usually lacks the paler spots towards the wing margins The forewings of both sexes are straight or slightly concave along the outer edge. The underside of the hindwings have a characteristic row of rust-red spots with silver centres, often bolder in the female. The tip of the forewing sometimes has two silvery spots, closer in from the margin.

**HABITAT:** Open woodland clearings and margins, scrubby limestone outcrops often underlaid with bracken.

**FREQUENCY:** Common in central Europe and parts of Fennoscandia, but becoming more local in the north-west, where in Britain it is the fastest declining Fritillary.

**LIFE HISTORY:** The fully formed caterpillar remains within its eggshell, hibernating for eight months. It hatches in early spring and immediately searches for nearby growths of violet. Typical of Fritillary caterpillars, it is fond of sunshine and basks on surrounding vegetation, being perfectly camouflaged at rest on dried bracken. The brown chrysalis is spotted with pearls of silver and is suspended in a loose tent of vegetation for three to four weeks. Adults appear in a single generation from June until August.

f. *cleodoxa* ♂

Very rarely specimens occur with the silver spots on the underside missing, form *cleodoxa*, though this is commoner further south.

LOOKALIKES

**Dark Green Fritillary** *Argynnis aglaja*
Wings more rounded, upperside of female paler towards the outer margins and more heavily edged in black. Undersides uniform blue-green and ochre. More widespread and often found in open countryside. (See p.100)

f. *eris* ♂

**Niobe Fritillary** *Argynnis niobe*
Similar to the High Brown Fritillary though usually smaller and with the sex-brands on veins 2 and 3 less prominent. Its flight and the shape of the wings however, are more like the Dark Green Fritillary. On the underside the veins are lined in black and the small pale spot at the base of the cell usually has a diagnostic black dot. Like the High Brown Fritillary, specimens commonly appear which lack the silver markings, form *eris*. It is single brooded and flies in July and August in light open woodlands and scrubby hillsides. Found throughout most of Europe, including parts of Fennoscandia, but not the British Isles.

*103*

# Queen of Spain Fritillary
*Issoria lathonia*

A beautiful butterfly, with typical Fritillary markings on elegantly curved forewings, especially lovely on the underside. Females are larger than males with a heavier suffusion of olive-green at the base of the wings. The large, silvery discs, surrounded by rust-red make it easy to identify as it feeds in flowery meadows and uncultivated places. It also spends much of its time basking on sun baked ground. A strong flyer, with an expanding range on the Continent, where, in the south and in parts of Scandinavia, it is a familiar and common species. In recent years, apart from a few migrants that arrive in Britain most years, there is some evidence of a resident population on the east coast. The caterpillar feeds on violets and pansies, and although winter is usually spent in this stage, it is thought that hibernation may occur in any stage of the life-cycle. In good years up to three generations may appear, flying from April until October.

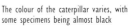

The colour of the caterpillar varies, with some specimens being almost black

# Lesser Marbled Fritillary

*Brenthis ino*

Widely distributed throughout central and eastern Europe and quite common in parts of Fennoscandia, this is a close relative of the larger Marbled Fritillary. It is best identified by the markings on the underside of the hindwings, which in this butterfly has a clear yellow patch where space 4 meets the cell. On the upperside the male's wings are less rounded but females are more difficult to separate as the intensity of the markings is variable. This butterfly prefers damp fertile habitats, with lush growths of wildflowers, particularly meadowsweet, the main foodplant of the caterpillar. The life-cycle is similar to other Fritillaries and hibernation is spent in the larval stage. There is one generation a year from June until August depending on the locality.

# Marbled Fritillary

*Brenthis daphne*

This medium sized Fritillary, found only in the south east of the region, can be recognised on the upperside, by its large rounded wings. The underside of the hindwings are very like the Lesser Marbled Fritillary but the central area, where space 4 meets the cell, is clouded with rusty-brown. It flies in open, scrubby woodland in a single generation from May until August, visiting the flowers of bramble, which is also the caterpillar's foodplant. Locally common in south eastern Europe.

# Pearl-bordered Fritillary

*Clossiana euphrosyne*

**M**ainly found in open woodlands, this is one of the first Fritillaries to appear on the wing in northern Europe. It has a rapid gliding flight and in early springtime it eagerly seeks nectar from bugle, primrose and other purple or yellow flowers, along open woodland rides. Earlier this century it was considered one of the commonest woodland butterflies in Britain but it has suffered a serious decline and is now found mainly in south western England, Wales, Scotland and the west coast of Ireland.

Pearl-bordered Fritillaries often visit the flowers of bugle to feed

| | |
|---|---|
| J | / |
| F | / |
| M | / |
| A | / ♦ 🦋 |
| M | • ♦ 🦋 |
| J | • / 🦋 |
| J | • / ♦ |
| A | • / ♦ 🦋 |
| S | / |
| O | / |
| N | / |
| D | / |

**KEY FEATURES:** The upperside ground-colour of the male is rich orange, with the larger female being slightly paler, particularly towards the margins. It is similar to but rather lighter than the Small Pearl-bordered Fritillary. The most reliable way of separating the uppersides of the two species is the row of post-discal spots on the forewings, particularly the spot in space 4. In the Pearl-bordered Fritillary it is mid-way between the two spots either side of it, whereas in the Small Pearl-bordered Fritillary it is nearer the margin. The underside of the hindwings is the easiest means of identification, the Pearl-bordered Fritillary having less contrast, only a small black spot in the middle of the cell and just one prominent silver spot in the centre of the wing.

**HABITAT:** Mainly in open or coppiced woodland, sunny sheltered glades with plenty of wild flowers.

**FREQUENCY:** Becoming rarer in Britain but locally common elsewhere, as far north as northern Fennoscandia.

**LIFE HISTORY:** Eggs are laid on or nearby various species of violet growing in warm sheltered places. The caterpillar hibernates from September until the following spring and continues feeding until late April, when it forms a chrysalis low down amongst the vegetation. The chrysalis lasts for about ten days and adults emerge to fly from late April until June and occasionally in a partial second brood in August.

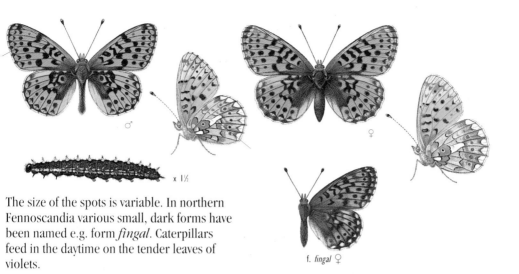

f. *fingal* ♀

The size of the spots is variable. In northern Fennoscandia various small, dark forms have been named e.g. form *fingal*. Caterpillars feed in the daytime on the tender leaves of violets.

## LOOKALIKES

**Bog Fritillary** *Proclossiana eunomia*
Upperside markings linear, with the post-discal areas of the forewings broad and containing an even, curved row of spots. The underside of the hindwings has a diagnostic row of six, white-centred spots. Becoming rare in France, Belgium and Germany but most wide-spread in Fennoscandia, where it occurs in boggy places in June and July. The caterpillar, which feeds on bistort, may take two seasons to complete its growth in the far north.

**Small Pearl-bordered Fritillary**
*Clossiana selene*
Upperside more fulvous-red and with the post-discal spot in space 4 of the forewings closer to the margins. On the underside the markings have more contrast. The veins are black and there is a prominent spot in the middle of the rust coloured cell. Usually appears later than the Pearl-bordered Fritillary but flight periods do over-lap. (See p.108)

# Small Pearl-bordered Fritillary

*Clossiana selene*

A butterfly mainly of damp woodland glades, often in the same habitats and flying with, the Pearl-bordered Fritillary. It has a rapid, low flight and visits a variety of springtime flowers, with a particular fondness for ragged robin, bird's foot trefoil and late flowering bugle. The first butterflies appear several weeks later than the Pearl-bordered Fritillary and so often look in fresher condition. Like other woodland Fritillaries it has declined, due to the cessation of coppicing and the loss of damp meadows and moorlands.

Male Small Pearl-bordered Fritillaries are attracted to many wild flowers, including creeping buttercup

x 1½

The caterpillar feeds on violets and is easily identified by the two spines on the first segment

| | | | |
|---|---|---|---|
| J | ✦ | | |
| F | ✦ | | |
| M | ✦ | | |
| A | ✦ ✦ | | |
| M | • | ✦ ✦ | 🦋 |
| J | • | ✦ ✦ | 🦋 |
| J | • | ✦ ✦ | 🦋 |
| A | • | ✦ ✦ | 🦋 |
| S | ✦ | | |
| O | ✦ | | |
| N | ✦ | | |
| D | ✦ | | |

**KEY FEATURES:** Slightly smaller than the Pearl-bordered Fritillary with the upperside of the male richer-fulvous. The undersides are the most reliable means of separating the two species, the Small Pearl-bordered Fritillary being much brighter with more contrast. The uppersides are usually more strongly marked around the edges and the post-discal spot in space 4 of the forewings is closer to the margin. (See p.106)

**HABITAT:** As well as sunny woodland glades, it occurs in more open places, such as coastal-cliffs, moorlands and damp, fertile meadows.

**FREQUENCY:** Widespread and locally common throughout Europe but scarce in eastern and central England and absent from Ireland.

**LIFE HISTORY:** The life-cycle follows a similar pattern to the Pearl-bordered Fritillary but is two weeks behind in each stage. The caterpillars of both species may be found together but the Small Pearl-bordered Fritillary is more secretive and less likely to be observed. The chrysalis is suspended, concealed amongst dried vegetation, and unlike the Pearl-bordered Fritillary, is adorned with bold silver spots. Usually only one generation occurs but in warm summers and further south, some butterflies may appear in August.

♀                                   f. hela ♀

Aberrations occasionally appear with enlarged spots merging together. In parts of Fennoscandia forms occur which are smaller and darker. E.g. form *hela*.

## Lookalikes

♂

♂

**Shepherd's Fritillary** *Boloria pales*
Uppersides of the sexes are similar, bright fulvous orange, strongly marked with black. Markings on the underside of the forewings, very faint. On the hindwing space 3, suffused. Flies in July and August on flowery slopes in the extreme south of Germany.

**Pearl-bordered Fritillary**
*Clossiana euphrosyne*
Paler and slightly larger, the post-discal spot in space 4 of the forewing is mid-way between the two spots either side. The underside is more ochreous with less contrast and fewer 'pearls'. (See above and p.106)

♂

♂

**Cranberry Fritillary** *Boloria aquilonaris*
Uppersides of the sexes are similar, bright fulvous red, with well developed markings. The discal spot in space 2 touches, or is close to, the cell vein. Markings on the underside of the forewings are well developed and diagnostic. The hindwings are rust red and in space 3 the post-discal spot is well developed, often with a pale centre. Widespread throughout Fennoscandia, south westward to Germany, with isolated colonies further west. On the wing from June until August.

♀

**Mountain Fritillary** *Boloria napaea*
Markings more linear and in space 2, the discal marking is usually away from the cell. Markings on the underside of the forewings, very faint, and on the hindwing, space 3 is clear yellow. Occurs in the extreme south of Germany but widely distributed in Fennoscandia, where it flies from June until August, often with the Cranberry Fritillary.

# LOOKALIKES

With more than thirty species of Fritillary found in the area covered by this book, confusion is possible, particularly with the uppersides. Identification is best made by studying the underside of the hindwings and when photographing Fritillaries, views of both surfaces should help in determining positive identification.

### Arctic Fritillary *Clossiana chariclea*

A rare butterfly, confined to the extreme north of Fennoscandia. The upperside is fulvous, strongly marked with black and heavily suffused near the wing bases. The row of chevrons around the edge of the wings, especially the hindwings, are very close to the margins. The underside of the hindwings are purple-brown with clear silver discal markings and a narrow silver marginal band. It flies over grassy mountain slopes in July. Restricted in its distribution, it can be locally common in places.

### Freyja's Fritillary *Clossiana freija*

In Europe, found only in Fennoscandia, where it is commoner in the northern bogs. The base of the wings on the upperside are heavily suffused with black, and on the forewings, the zig-zag discal band is characteristic. There is a zig-zag band on the underside of the hindwings, which also have a marginal row of arrow-shaped lunules. The sexes are similar, though the female is slightly larger and paler. It flies in early June, often in the company of the Pearl-bordered Fritillary.

### Polar Fritillary *Clossiana polaris*

Restricted to the rocky tundra of northern Fennoscandia, where it occasionally flies with the Arctic Fritillary. The uppersides of both sexes are fulvous yellow, with a heavy suffusion of black at the base of the wings. The underside of the hindwings are dark reddish-brown with strongly contrasting silver spots, those along the margins forming a regular row of 'T' shaped markings. It flies in one generation from June until August.

### Frigga's Fritillary *Clossiana frigga*

Found locally in wet, scrubby habitats of Fennoscandia, sometimes flying with the Bog and Pearl-bordered Fritillaries. It is evenly marked with strong black spots on the upperside, though these markings vary according to the locality. Sexes are similar, the female slightly darker. The underside of the hindwings is distinctive, with the outer half being weakly suffused with pale violet. The main flight period is July.

ssp *cypris*

**Titania's Fritillary** *Clossiana titania*
Found in widely separated populations throughout
Europe, the largest in southern Finland and the Alps.
The female is slightly larger than the male, both are well
marked on the uppersides, with characteristic pointed
triangles around the margins. These are repeated on
the underside of the hindwings, where they touch the
inner row of post-discal spots. The undersides are
attractively marbled with rust-brown, ochre and violet,
which is much bolder in the Alpine sub-species *cypris*.
The caterpillar feeds on bistort, adults fly from June
until August`

**Weaver's Fritillary** *Clossiana dia*
Distributed throughout central and eastern Europe but
absent from Britain and Fennoscandia, this is one of the
smallest of the Fritillaries, resembling a dwarf Titania's
Fritillary sub-species *cypris*. The hindwing has a
distinctively sharp apex, similar to that of the Boloria
Fritillaries and on the underside it is heavily marbled
with rust-brown and deep violet. It flies in woodland
clearings and valleys from April until September in two
broods.

ssp *borealis* ♂

**Thor's Fritillary** *Clossiana thore*
In Europe, found only in the Alps as far north as Bavaria
and in Fennoscandia, where specimens are paler and
less heavily marked, sub-species *borealis*. Typically, it is
the darkest *Clossiana* Fritillary, rich-orange, heavily
marked and suffused with black. The underside of the
hindwings have a clear greenish-yellow discal band and
a narrow, silvery marginal line. It flies on open mountainsides as well as clearings in pine and birch woodlands,
from June until August, depending on the locality.

**Dusky-winged Fritillary** *Clossiana improba*
The smallest and dullest Fritillary, which, in Europe
occurs only in northern Fennoscandia. Its size, distribution
and dusky appearance, make it unlikely to be confused
with any other butterfly. It flies low to the ground on
grassy mountain slopes, sometimes in company with the
Arctic Fritillary. Adults fly in July but little is known
about the rest of its life-cycle.

# Glanville Fritillary

*Melitaea cinxia*

A butterfly of sunny, flowery meadows and hillsides on the continent but in Britain confined to the southern coast of the Isle of Wight, where it rarely ventures far from the undercliffs. It is a graceful sun-loving insect, fond of gliding from flower to flower and with a particular liking for bird's foot trefoil. In Britain it had several English names before the Glanville Fritillary, including the Lincolnshire Fritillary and Plantain Fritillary but its present name comes from Lady Eleanor Glanville who discovered it about 300 years ago.

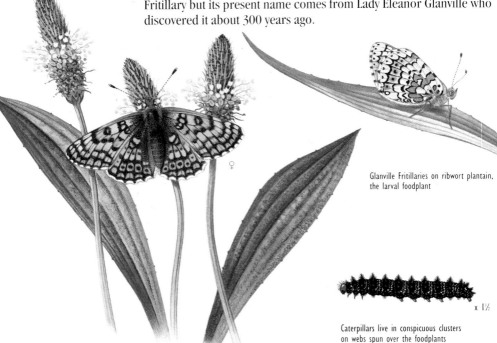

Glanville Fritillaries on ribwort plantain, the larval foodplant

x 1½

Caterpillars live in conspicuous clusters on webs spun over the foodplants

| | |
|---|---|
| J | ✔ |
| F | ✔ |
| M | ✔ |
| A | ✔ ▶ |
| M | · ▶ 🦋 |
| J | · ✔ 🦋 |
| J | · ✔ 🦋 |
| A | ✔ |
| S | ✔ |
| O | ✔ |
| N | ✔ |
| D | ✔ |

**KEY FEATURES:** Both sexes are evenly banded with black and the hindwings have a characteristic row of post-discal spots. On the underside, the tips of the forewings and the margins of the hindwings have rounded spots. The yellow post-discal band on the hindwings, contain a row of orange spots with black centres, these orange spots lack a black internal border, characteristic of the Knapweed Fritillary.

**HABITAT:** Varied, sunny, uncultivated ground and scrubby, wooded hills with plenty of flowers. In Britain it is restricted to crumbling undercliffs and chines of the Isle of Wight.

**FREQUENCY:** Widespread and quite common in central Europe and southern Fennoscandia.

**LIFE HISTORY:** Batches of 50 to over 200 yellow eggs are laid on the underside of plantain leaves. On hatching the small caterpillars form a communal web over the foodplant and continue to feed and bask in the sun until the Autumn. They then enter into hibernation within the conspicuous web and remain concealed until the following March. Growth is completed by late April and the chrysalis is formed, hidden amongst low vegetation. The first butterflies emerge in May and the flight period lasts until mid July, though further south two generations may appear.

The ground colour of the male is light orange with the female more ochreous.

## LOOKALIKES

**Knapweed Fritillary** *Melitaea phoebe*
A variable butterfly, typical specimens are heavily marked and with a more variegated orange ground colour. On the forewings, the orange marginal crescent in space 3 is large and indented and on the hindwings the post-discal band may or may not have small spots. The black marginal markings on the underside, are linear and the orange spots in the post-discal band, have black internal borders and no central spot. Fairly common in flowery scrub-land in central and southern Europe, absent from the north. Flies from April until August in up to three broods, depending on locality.

**Spotted Fritillary** *Melitaea didyma*
The deep orange ground colour of the male, with clear spots rather than bands, should quickly identify this butterfly. There are also conspicuous orange scales around the head and the tip of the abdomen which is banded with white. The female is more variable. The ground colour is paler with more suffused darker markings, sometimes obscuring nearly all the orange. The underside of both sexes is similar and distinctive with the orange forming two clear, continuous bands on a cream ground colour, which is boldly spotted with black. A common central European butterfly, with a similar distribution to the Knapweed Fritillary, it flies from May until September in up to three broods.

**Heath Fritillary** *Mellicta athalia*
Orange ground colour deeper, with heavier black markings near the wing bases. Post-discal spots of the hindwings absent. The underside of the hindwings have a broad pale discal band and the marginal markings are linear. There are no post-discal spots. (See p.114)

# Heath Fritillary

*Mellicta athalia*

The commonest and most widely distributed of the *Mellicta* Fritillaries, it is also the most variable and in central Europe, is easily confused with its near relatives. In southern Britain, at the extreme north-west of its range, its numbers have greatly declined this century, due mainly to changes in woodland management. These include the cessation of coppicing, resulting in woodlands becoming overgrown, and the introduction of large numbers of game birds, that decimate the caterpillars.

The amount of black varies between individuals. Males are often darker orange and less variegated than females

| | |
|---|---|
| J | ✔ |
| F | ✔ |
| M | ✔ |
| A | ✔ |
| M | ✔ ✔ |
| J | • ✔ ✔ 🦋 |
| J | • ✔ ✔ 🦋 |
| A | • ✔ 🦋 |
| S | ✔ |
| O | ✔ |
| N | ✔ |
| D | ✔ |

**KEY FEATURES:** Usually the largest of the *Mellictas*, though sizes vary. The upperside is clear orange, more variegated in the female and boldly marked with black. The underside of the forewings has a prominent dark mark in space 2. The hindwings are very similar to the four species opposite, where distinguishing features are described.

**HABITAT:** Open glades and coppiced woodland, rough grassy slopes with plenty of wild flowers.

**FREQUENCY:** Common throughout central and northern Europe including southern Fennoscandia. In England, local in Kent and the West Country.

**LIFE HISTORY:** The eggs are laid in batches, under the leaves of cow-wheat, plantain or speedwell and more rarely on other plants. The young caterpillars live in small groups, in webs spun amongst the foodplants. They hibernate in the autumn and reappear the following spring, completing their growth in May, having spent eleven months in the larval stage. The chrysalis is concealed, suspended amongst dried vegetation, close to the ground where it remains for about two weeks. The butterfly is on the wing from June until August in the north but further south, it may occur in two broods, lasting from April until September.

x 1½

# LOOKALIKES

Observations of both surfaces are necessary for positive identification of the Heath Fritillary and the next four species.

Perhaps the most variable European butterfly, collected in large numbers by Victorian butterfly collectors hoping for extreme aberrations. The caterpillar, like other Fritillaries, spends much of its time basking in the sun.

**Meadow Fritillary** *Mellicta parthenoides*
Black markings on the upperside are linear, leaving the post-discal area comparatively clear, with discal markings often bolder. The discal area towards the costal margin of the hindwings, is also clear. The underside is variable and similar to the Heath Fritillary. Found south of a line from Normandy to southern Germany.

**Nickerl's Fritillary** *Mellicta aurelia*
Black markings on the upperside complete, giving an even chequer-board pattern. On the underside of the hindwings, the narrow marginal band is slightly darker than the lunules inside it. Found in western, central and eastern France, Belgium and Germany.

**False Heath Fritillary** *Melitaea diamina*
The darkest of the 'chequered' fritillaries, with the yellow marginal markings of some specimens, reduced to small spots. On the underside of the hindwings, the post-discal lunules have characteristic black centres, edged with yellow and bordered internally with black. The narrow marginal band is yellow. Found in southern Fennoscandia, western and eastern France, Belgium and Germany, westwards.

**Assmann's Fritillary** *Mellicta britomartis*
Black markings on the upperside heavy, giving a darker appearance, even in flight. The outer rows of orange markings form even, double bands along the borders of all wings. On the underside of the hindwings, the orange post-discal lunules are heavily edged with black, and the narrow marginal band is darker and more ochreous than the lunules inside it. Found only in south-eastern Sweden in the region covered by this book, in eastern Europe it may be rather brighter.

# Marsh Fritillary

*Euphydryas aurinia*

Once known as the Greasy Fritillary, because of the appearance of slightly worn specimens, this butterfly, like so many other species that occur in wetland habitats, is threatened with extinction in many European localities. Because of its drastic decline it is protected throughout much of Europe, though ironically not in Britain, where sites are still being destroyed with governmental approval. It does occur in drier habitats than its name suggests and colonies exist on some quite dry downland sites.

The meadow thistle is a favourite nectar source of the Marsh Fritillary

x 1½

Caterpillars are most easy to find after hibernation

| | |
|---|---|
| J | ✓ |
| F | ✓ |
| M | ✓ |
| A | ✓ ♪ |
| M | · ♪ 🦋 |
| J | · ✓ ♪ 🦋 |
| J | · ✓ 🦋 |
| A | ✓ |
| S | ✓ |
| O | ✓ |
| N | ✓ |
| D | ✓ |

**KEY FEATURES:** The tri-coloured chequered appearance is distinctive, with some specimens, notably those in Ireland, being particularly beautifully marked, form *hibernica*. On the hindwings, the black spots in the broad orange post-discal band are diagnostic.

**HABITAT:** Damp flowery clearings in woodlands, wet meadows, sunny downland slopes with an abundance of wild flowers.

**FREQUENCY:** In favourable places it can be abundant but populations can be dramatically influenced by parasitic *Apanteles* wasps. Many sites have been destroyed by drainage of marshes for agricultural development, peat abstraction and open cast mining etc.

**LIFE HISTORY:** The egg batch is laid on the underside leaves of devil's bit scabious, growing in a sheltered warm situation. Newly hatched caterpillars are gregarious and live in a conspicuous web, spun amongst the foodplant. They move about, constructing further webs rather like Small Tortoiseshells, and in the autumn reinforce the structure ready for hibernation. They emerge in the early spring sunshine, when they are at their most conspicuous, and continue to feed and bask together until fully grown. They then disperse and live alone prior to pupation, having spent the last ten months as a caterpillar. The attractive white, black and orange chrysalis is formed suspended amongst vegetation, where it remains for about two weeks. Butterflies emerge in May and are on the wing until July

Most individuals vary slightly from specimen to specimen but extreme aberrations are rare. Females are generally larger, though small specimens of both sexes sometimes occur.

♀ Irish form *hibernica*

## LOOKALIKES

**Scarce Fritillary** *Hypodryas maturna*
A larger and brighter species with a deep orange ground colour and without spots in the post-discal band of the hindwings. The upperside is variable, with some specimens having broad orange post-discal bands and others being dark, with the pale markings almost white. A beautiful insect, which flies in wet woodland clearings, where its caterpillar feeds, unusually for a Fritillary, on ash, poplar and aspen, and then on various low herbs after hibernation. As its name implies it is rare and declining, found in southern Sweden and Finland, parts of central France and Germany, eastwards.

**Lapland Fritillary** *Hypodryas iduna*
More heavily marked than the Marsh Fritillary and with more contrast between the orange and cream bands. It lacks the post-discal spots on the hindwings, and on the underside it is bolder with black venation. A local butterfly, restricted to marshy scrub in northern Fennoscandia, where it flies in June and July. The caterpillar feeds on plantain and speedwells.

**Heath Fritillary** *Mellicta athelia*
Upperside deeper orange and evenly chequered with black bands. The hindwings lack the post-discal row of spots. On the underside there is more contrast, with the veins and all markings of the hindwings outlined in black. (See p.114)

# Marbled White
## *Melanargia galathea*

A distinct and attractive butterfly whose lazy flapping flight is characteristic of rough flowery downland, where it vies for nectar on knapweeds and thistles with Chalkhill Blues and Skipper butterflies. Sometimes mistaken by the novice for a member of the Pierid or 'White' family, it is in fact a Satyrid or 'Brown'. It is the only one of seven species of European 'Marbled White' found in the north.

The upperside of the female is greyer than the male and the front edge of the forewings are ochreous towards the bases. On the underside, the hindwings are more ochreous grey. The caterpillar rests low down in grass tussocks in the daytime and emerges to feed at night.

x 2¼

**KEY FEATURES:** The black and white chequering make it unmistakable in northern Europe.

**HABITAT:** Uncultivated places with an abundance of flowers, sunny woodland rides and uncut roadside verges, chalk and limestone downland.

**FREQUENCY:** Common and often abundant in many places throughout central Europe but often absent from apparently suitable habitats.

**LIFE HISTORY:** The eggs are laid randomly, dropped into the grass, as the female perches and flutters amongst the vegetation. Soon after emerging, the young caterpillar enters hibernation in dried grasses. It starts feeding again the following spring, on various grasses, including sheep's fescue, red fescue and tor grass. It feeds at night and is found in two colour forms, either pale green or buff with a dark stripe down the back. By June it is fully grown after eleven months as a caterpillar, it then pupates on the ground and the chrysalis lasts for two to three weeks before the adult butterfly emerges.

J /
F /
M /
A /
M /
J / ▸ ✖
J · / ▸ ✖
A · / ✖
S /
O /
N /
D /

# Woodland Grayling
*Hipparchia fagi*

# Rock Grayling
*Hipparchia alcyone*

These two butterflies can only be separated for certainty by locality or examination of the genitalia. There are certain external characters which can help identification but these may not be constant.

The **Woodland Grayling** (above, left and below left) is larger, with the pale post-discal band of the forewings suffused with brown and the hindwings lighter. The female is bigger than the male with broader, brighter markings. The undersides are so variable that no reliable characters can be used for identification. Butterflies are on the wing from June until August, in lightly wooded countryside, up to 1,000m. They often rest, concealed on tree trunks, and males will fly boldly to confront even small birds that fly into their territory. The caterpillar feeds on various grasses including, upright brome and tor grass. It is buff coloured, with faint striations along the sides and a broken dorsal stripe. Locally distributed throughout central Europe as far north as central Germany, absent from Britain and Fennoscandia.

The **Rock Grayling** (above right and right) is smaller, the length of the forewing being on average 3–4mm less than the Woodland Graylings. The post-discal bands tend to be creamier and more clearly defined. Butterflies are on the wing from late June until August, occurring on warm, sparsely vegetated, mountain slopes, up to 1,500m. The caterpillar feeds on grasses including, sheep's fescue and tor grass. It is buff coloured with striations along the sides and a continuous black, dorsal stripe. Local and less widely distributed, it occurs in central and eastern France, eastwards and in an isolated population in southern Norway, where the Woodland Grayling does not occur.

**The Hermit** *Chazara briseis*

Rare in northern Europe, with isolated populations in France and Germany, more widespread further south. The irregular post-discal bands are clearly defined and dusky-cream in the male. The female is larger with broader white bands and a buff costal margin to the forewings. On the undersides, the hindwings are sexually dimophic and are unlike any other species in the region. Flies throughout the summer months on dry grassy slopes, where the caterpillar feeds on grasses, including upright brome.

**Great Banded Grayling** *Kanetisa circe*

Equal in size, or even larger than the Woodland Grayling, the ground colour is darker and the bands are whiter and more clearly defined, a feature noticeable in flight. The underside is beautifully variegated, with diagnostic white splashes within the discal areas. Widely distributed and quite common in parts of central Europe, extending as far north as southern Germany. It flies from June until August, in warm open woodland and scrub, where it often alights on tree trunks. The caterpillar feeds at night on various grasses.

# Grayling
*Hipparchia semele*

Amaster of camouflage, the Grayling occurs in a variety of habitats which are often reflected in the underside markings of its wings. On heathland for example, specimens are much darker than those that live on chalk or limestone hills. It prefers open, sparsely vegetated places, where it can conceal itself on the stony ground and angle itself to the sun to regulate its temperature. Unlike most butterflies, the Grayling is not an avid flower feeder, though it sometimes visits heathers, thyme or other purple blooms, when the weather is warm and dry.

LOOKALIKES

x 1½

The caterpillar is sluggish and feeds at night on various species of grass

♂

♀

**KEY FEATURES:** In southern Europe there are several very similar, closely related species, but in the area covered by this book, the Grayling is fairly easily recognised. The upperside is hardly ever seen, as the butterfly always settles with its wings closed. The underside of the forewings are sometimes exposed but when lowered, just the mottled hindwing and the tip of the forewing are visible.

**HABITAT:** Found in dry sunny places, from sea level to mountain slopes and on soil ranging from acidic heathland to chalk and limestone downs.

**FREQUENCY:** Common throughout most of Europe, in Britain and Fennoscandia it is mainly coastal.

**LIFE HISTORY:** The white egg is laid on or near small tussocks of various species of grass, including, sheep's fescue, bristle bent and tufted hair-grass. It hatches after two to three weeks and the young caterpillar enters hibernation when it is about 1cm in length. On mild winter nights it may emerge to feed but full activity does not start until the spring. Like the adult butterfly, the caterpillar is perfectly concealed when resting amongst dried vegetation. Pupation takes place just below ground, in a cell constructed by the caterpillar (see p.14). The rust-red chrysalis lasts for a month and butterflies begin to appear at the end of June, the flight period lasting until September.

# Lookalikes

### Tree Grayling *Neohipparchia statilinus*
The underside, which is the surface most often seen, is variable but with less contrast than the grayling. The two conspicuous eye-spots on the forewings are ringed with yellow and have two diagnostic white spots between them. Flies in dry stony scrub and open woodland from July until September. Mainly southern and eastern European distribution where it can be common. Local in north western France but disappearing from several central European countries.

### False Grayling *Arethusana arethusa*
Often settles with its wings open, the underside of this butterfly has more evenly granular markings, with a clearly defined submarginal line on both wings. The veins on the hindwings are pale in some specimens. Uppersides of both sexes have a broken post-discal band of orange across all wings, which may sometimes be reduced to spots. On the wing from July until September, flying on chalk grassland, heaths and scrubland, in central and eastern France.

### Dryad *Minois dryas*
Characterised by two large, blue centred spots on both sides of the forewings, and a smaller spot on the hind-wings, which have distinctive scalloped margins. Male is much smaller and darker than the female; on the under-side of the hindwings, he usually lacks the contrast between the basal and outer half of the wings. Local in central France and southern Germany, it flies from July until September in open woodland and grassy scrub.

All the European species of *Oeneis*, except *Oeneis glacialis*, occur only in Fennoscandia, in the area covered by this book.

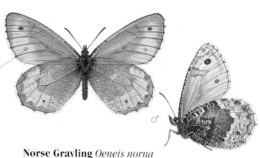

### Norse Grayling *Oeneis norna*

Closely resembles the Arctic Grayling but the ground colour is less grey and with distinctly paler post-discal bands. Spots on the forewings are sometimes very small, usually more prominent in spaces 2 and 5. Sexes similar. Flies in June and July on rocky moorland and birch scrub. Mainly in northern Fennoscandia, local further south to central Norway.

### Arctic Grayling *Oeneis bore*

Paler than the Norse Grayling and without post-discal spots, worn specimens can appear virtually unmarked. The upperside of the forewings of both sexes have only faint, post-discal bands. Sexes similar. It is a rarer butterfly, restricted to the barren mountain slopes of northern Fennoscandia, where it flies in June and July.

### Alpine Grayling *Oeneis glacialis*

Usually slightly darker than the Norse Grayling, with broader marginal bands. Sexes are similar, though the female often has bold eye-spots on all wings, these may be absent in the male. The underside of the hindwings have characteristic white veins. As its common name suggests, it is an Alpine butterfly, venturing just into southern Germany. It flies on rocky mountain slopes from June until August.

### Baltic Grayling *Oeneis jutta*

Quite common in parts of central and eastern Fennoscandia, it is noticeably darker than related species, with a slatey blue tone to the underside of the hindwings. Sexes similar. It flies in sparse, pine scattered moorland in June and July.

# Scotch Argus
*Erebia aethiops*

This member of the large *Erebia* group, with nearly 50 European species, is one of only two that occur in Britain. It is a sun loving butterfly, basking and flying on warm days and resting concealed in the vegetation when the sun disappears. Its flight is low and unhurried, with males inspecting dead leaves and any other dark objects, in the hope of finding a female. When freshly emerged, the male in particular, is a handsome insect, with the deep velvet-brown wings, contrasting with rust-red bands and eye-spots.

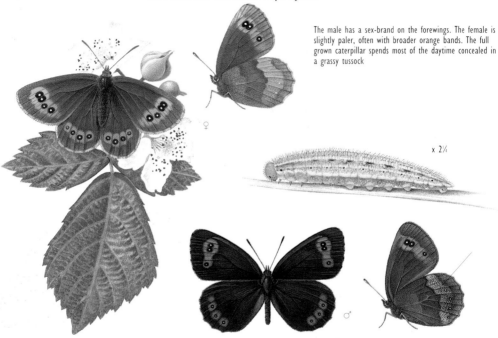

The male has a sex-brand on the forewings. The female is slightly paler, often with broader orange bands. The full grown caterpillar spends most of the daytime concealed in a grassy tussock

x 2¼

♀

♂

| | |
|---|---|
| J | ✓ |
| F | ✓ |
| M | ✓ |
| A | ✓ |
| M | ✓ |
| J | ✓ ✓ |
| J | ✓ 🦋 |
| A | · ✓ ✓ 🦋 |
| S | · ✓ 🦋 |
| O | ✓ |
| N | ✓ |
| D | ✓ |

**KEY FEATURES:** The size of the orange bands on the upperside varies but the black spots usually have white centres on all wings. Wing fringes are indistinctly chequered. The underside of the hindwings is diagnostic, with two dark and two light bands, the post-discal one being the brightest.

**HABITAT:** Damp moorland, heaths and grassy hillsides, scattered with pine trees.

**FREQUENCY:** Common in the Alps but more localised further north, though it may be abundant in some localities.

**LIFE HISTORY:** Like all *Erebias*, the eggs are laid on various species of grass or sedge, the Scotch Argus often favouring purple moor grass. On hatching, the small caterpillar feeds for about a month, and in October enters hibernation for the next five months. It continues feeding, mainly at night, for a further three months, when it pupates in June, concealed on the ground at the base of the foodplant. Butterflies emerge about two weeks later and are on the wing from July until September in a single brood.

# LOOKALIKES

The *Erebias* are one of the largest and most confusing genera of European butterflies. Mainly occurring in the Pyrenees and the Alps, the cut off line for many species is the southern border of Germany.

**Arran Brown** *Erebia ligea*
Male with a sex-brand on forewings. Upperside, red bands often broad, wing fringes conspicuously chequered black and white. The underside of the hindwings have the outer margin of the discal area edged in white, boldest near the costa, sometimes reduced to a few white spots. Three of four black post-discal spots are usually present. Common throughout Fennoscandia, eastern France and southern Germany, flying in July and August.

**Large Ringlet** *Erebia euryale*
Male without a sex-brand on forewings. Like the Arran Brown but the black eye-spots are usually small and blind. Underside of male hindwings dark, with an indication of a pale post-discal band and an obscure white mark in space 4. Female has a paler post-discal area, sometimes with a few small spots. Found locally in southern Germany and eastern France in July and August.

**Lapland Ringlet** *Erebia embla*
Found only in central and northern Fennoscandia, the sexes are similar, with four yellow-ringed spots on the forewings, the top two larger, often with white centres. The hindwings also have two to four eye-spots. The underside of the hindwings are dark, with the post-discal area only slightly paler and with a row of small spots. Flies in June and July

**Arctic Ringlet** *Erebia disa*
Found only in northern Fennoscandia, it is slightly paler than the Lapland Ringlet, with the orange on the forewings forming a continuous band and enclosing smaller blind spots. The hindwings have no spots. The underside of the hindwings have more contrast and in the outer half, the markings form a distinct wavy line. Flies in June and July.

**Woodland Ringlet** *Erebia medusa*
Four to six black spots on each forewing, with those in spaces 2, 4 and 5 the largest and with white centres. The orange rings, surrounding the spots in spaces 4 and 5 are elongated internally. The pattern is repeated on the underside, which is characteristically uniform brown on the hindwings. Widespread from eastern France, southern Belgium and central southern Germany, eastwards. Flight period from May until July.

**Arctic Woodland Ringlet** *Erebia polaris*
Found only in northern Norway and Finland, where it flies in damp coastal meadows in June and July. Once regarded as a sub-species of the Woodland Ringlet it resembles a smaller version, with duller markings. The underside of the hindwings is sometimes slightly paler in the outer half.

**Bright-eyed Ringlet** *Erebia oeme*
The upperside of the forewings has two small but prominent eye-spots in an elongated orange patch. The hindwings have a row of 3 or 4 spots, evenly ringed with orange. On the underside the markings are repeated, those on the hindwings being altogether brighter. Occurring just into southern Germany, where it flies in damp meadows and woodlands from June until August.

**Piedmont Ringlet** *Erebia meolans*
Orange markings of the forewings taper evenly towards apex, and on the hindwings, the orange extends inwards from the black eye-spots. The undersides of the forewings of both sexes are diagnostic, having broad, orange post-discal bands. The hindwings are paler in the outer halves. Found on flowery hillsides in eastern France and southern Germany, when it is on the wing in June and July.

**Marbled Ringlet** *Erebia montana*
Underside hindwings of both sexes mottled with white, female with more orange and distinctly chequered wing fringes. An Alpine Ringlet, flying in late summer, and just reaching southern Germany.

# Mountain Ringlet
*Erebia epiphron*

Found mainly in the mountains of southern and eastern Europe, where it is variable and has many sub-species. Populations also occur in northern Britain, where it is the only true Alpine butterfly, restricted to the mountains of the Lake District and Scotland. It is an unspectacular little butterfly that often goes unnoticed on dull days but when the sun shines, adults may appear abundantly on warm, grassy, mountain slopes. Males are more often encountered, flying low over mat-grass in search of the heavy, egg laden females.

♂

♀

The female is slightly paler than the male with broader orange markings

x 2¼

Female feeding from tormentil

**KEY FEATURES:** Easily identified in Britain, in the rest of Europe, especially the Alps there are many similar species. Specimens occurring in southern Germany resemble those from Britain, with black spots reduced and sometimes absent in space 3. On the underside of the hindwings the basal area is sometimes slightly darker. In the mountains of eastern France specimens are more brightly marked and have bolder black spots.

**HABITAT:** Moorland and grassy mountain slopes to 1,000m and more.

**FREQUENCY:** Widely distributed throughout the mountainous regions of Europe, where it can be locally abundant, with colonies sometimes containing thousands of individuals.

**LIFE HISTORY:** The egg is laid singly amongst tussocks of mat grass, where it remains for two to three weeks. After hatching and eating its eggshell, the small caterpillar feeds until September, and then enters hibernation for the next six months. Feeding continues in the spring and it is full grown by the end of May. It feeds at night, and in the daytime the green and white stripes help conceal it in the grass, where it pupates, close to the ground, in a loose silken shelter. The chrysalis lasts for three weeks and the butterfly is on the wing from June until August in a single brood.

| | | | |
|---|---|---|---|
| J | ✓ | | |
| F | ✓ | | |
| M | ✓ | | |
| A | ✓ | ❯ | |
| M | ✓ | ❯ | |
| J | | ❯ | 🦋 |
| J | • | ❯ | 🦋 |
| A | • | ✓ | 🦋 |
| S | | ✓ | |
| O | | ✓ | |
| N | | ✓ | |
| D | | ✓ | |

# LOOKALIKES

**Eriphyle Ringlet** *Erebia eriphyle*
Found locally, on damp, flowery mountain slopes over 1,200m, in the Alps and just into southern Germany. The orange markings are well in from the margins, with small spots on the forewings in spaces 4, 5 and sometimes 2. On the hindwings the orange spot in space 4 is always the most prominent. The orange on the underside of the forewings extends into the discal area and on the hindwings, the unevenly spaced spots, lack black centres. Flies in July.

**Blind Ringlet** *Erebia pharte*
The orange markings on the upperside of the forewings form an even band, those on the hindwings an even row of spots. All are without black spots and are the same on the underside. Sexes are similar, the underside of the female being slightly paler. Found on flowery Alpine slopes in July.

**Yellow-spotted Ringlet** *Erebia manto*
Male similar to the Eriphyle Ringlet. The orange spots on the forewings are variable but those in spaces 4 and 5 are elongate, with black centres. On the underside, the post-discal markings form a clear band, with those in spaces 4 to 6 on the hindwings being the boldest. The underside of the female is easier to identify, the hindwing markings ranging from bright yellow, to white, in some specimens from the Vosges Mountains of eastern France. The males from this region have broad, orange, and usually spotless, bands. Shares a similar distribution as the Mountain Ringlet, excluding Britain.

## Lesser Mountain Ringlet *Erebia melampus*

Forewings of male are rounded, the orange band is broken by dark veins and the black spots get smaller from spaces 4 and 5. The hindwings have clear orange spots with black centres on both sides. The female is similar, though slightly paler. Flies in July and August on Alpine slopes as far north as southern Germany.

## Mnestra's Ringlet *Erebia mnestra*

This rare Alpine Ringlet flies in July, on grassy mountain slopes in southern Germany. The broad orange post-discal band of the male usually lacks the black spots in spaces 4 and 5 but these are normally present in the female. The orange often extends into the discal area on the upperside of the forewings and on the underside the whole discal and basal areas are tawny orange. The hindwings are plain, often with a slightly paler post-discal area.

## Silky Ringlet *Erebia gorge*

The common name comes from the texture of the orange forewing bands, which are smooth and usually have two white pupiled eye-spots. These are repeated on the underside, where the discal and basal areas are tawny orange. The hindwings are the best means of identification, being granular and with a contrasting dark discal band. Variable throughout the Alps and other mountain ranges. Flies from June to August, over rocky slopes exceeding 1500m.

## Dewy Ringlet *Erebia pandrose*

The tawny markings of the forewings extend into the discal area where they are crossed by darker lines. The row of black spots is sometimes indistinct but they are always without white pupils. The undersides of the hindwings, and tips of the forewings, are pale greyish, granular, and with the discal area outlined with wavy black bands. It is common in the central mountains of Norway and Sweden from north to south and throughout the Alps, where it flies over damp, scrubby mountain slopes from June until August.

# Meadow Brown
## Maniola jurtina

This common butterfly of rough grassy places, is familiar throughout Europe, except northern Fennoscandia and high mountains. It has a dancing, unhurried flight when visiting flowers but when alarmed is capable of strong, fast bursts. At rest, the cryptically coloured underside, helps in its camouflage, and the bold eye-spots act as decoys before being concealed behind the hindwings. Associated with sunny hay meadows in high summer, it is however, one of the few butterflies that flies on dull overcast days.

Males and females frequently feed from bramble flowers

The caterpillar is covered in long white hairs

x 2/1

| | | | |
|---|---|---|---|
| J | ✦ | | |
| F | ✦ | | |
| M | ✦ | | |
| A | ✦ | | |
| M | ✦ ✦ | | |
| J | · ✦ ✦ | ✺ | |
| J | · ✦ ✦ | ✺ | |
| A | · ✦ ✦ | ✺ | |
| S | · ✦ | ✺ | |
| O | · ✦ | | |
| N | ✦ | | |
| D | ✦ | | |

**KEY FEATURES:** The male is dark brown, with a black sex-brand below the cell on the forewings. The single black eye-spot has a white pupil and is surrounded by orange, which, in some specimens extends down into the post-discal area. Females are larger and brighter, with the orange often extending into the hindwings. The discal area on the underside of the hindwings is darker, with greater contrast in the female.

**HABITAT:** Wide ranging, including overgrown roadside verges, waste ground, woodland clearings, heaths and downland. Prefers taller, flower rich grasslands on all soil types.

**FREQUENCY:** One of the commonest European butterflies.

**LIFE HISTORY:** The small eggs are laid or dropped amongst grasses, the caterpillar feeding on various species, including meadow grass, bent and rye-grass. The young caterpillar feeds by day and although it becomes dormant in the winter, on mild days it continues to feed. The following spring it starts to feed at night and can be easily found, by torchlight. The chrysalis is formed suspended from a silken pad amongst the vegetation, it is variable in its colour and markings, depending on the surrounding background (see p.14). It lasts for about a month and the butterflies appear in a single generation, which extend from June until September.

♂

♀

The small black spots on the underside of the hindwings vary in size and have been the subject of study into evolutionary genetics.

## Lookalikes

♂

♂

**Gatekeeper** *Pyronia tithonus*
Smaller and brighter orange on all wings, interrupted by prominent sex-brands in the male. The eye-spots on the forewings are twin pupiled. The underside of the hindwings is reddish-brown and ochre, with white pupiled spots. Often flies in the company of the Meadow Brown but appears brighter even in flight. (See p.132)

♀

♂

**Dusky Meadow Brown** *Maniola lycaon*
Paler than the Meadow Brown, the sex-brands of the male are narrow and broken by veins 2 and 3. Both sexes have black eye-spots, often bold in the female, which lack the white pupils on the upperside. The males forewings have a yellow flush, but in the female this is clearer and brighter, extending into the hindwings. The undersides of the hindwings are variable, greyish, with the discal area edged with a darker wavy line. Mainly a southern and eastern European species, found only in southern Finland in the area covered by this book. Flies over scrubby, stony ground, June to August.

**Ringlet** *Aphantopus hyperantus*
The upperside resembles a fresh, male Meadow Brown but there is no trace of orange on either surface, giving a dark impression, even in flight. The 'ringlets' on both sides are distinguishing features when the two species fly together. (See p.133)

# Gatekeeper

*Pyronia tithonus*

Once known as the Hedge Brown, the Gatekeeper is common in many places throughout Europe but does not occur further north than northern England. It frequents sheltered hedgerows and woodland glades where it feeds avidly on the nectar of brambles and other flowers, basking in the sun between feeds.

The open flower-heads of ragwort often attract Gatekeepers in late summer

x 2¼

| | |
|---|---|
| J | ✓ |
| F | ✓ |
| M | ✓ |
| A | ✓ |
| M | ✓ |
| J | ✓ ▸ |
| J | · ▸ 🦋 |
| A | · ✓ ▸ 🦋 |
| S | ✓ ▸ 🦋 |
| O | ✓ |
| N | ✓ |
| D | ✓ |

**KEY FEATURES:** Conspicuous curved sex-brands cross the forewings of the male, whose ground colour is slightly richer than the female. Both sexes have twin pupiled eye-spots, some specimens having additional spots below these. The white pupils on the underside of the hindwings, distinguishes this butterfly from all others in the region.

**HABITAT:** Rough, grassy lanes and open woodland glades with shrubs and wild flowers.

**FREQUENCY:** Widely distributed and common, though its numbers vary from year to year.

**LIFE HISTORY:** The eggs are laid or dropped by the female amongst grasses, growing in sheltered places, along lanes or near bushes. The caterpillar may feed on various species of grass, including, meadow grass, timothy, couch and fescues. It feeds in the daytime whilst small but after hibernation feeds at night. There are two colour forms, green or brown and the chrysalis, which is white striped with brown, is suspended amongst dried vegetation near the ground. The flight period is from mid-July until early September.

LOOKALIKES: see Meadow Brown. (See p.130)

# Ringlet

*Aphantopus hyperantus*

Newly emerged male Ringlets have a deep, velvety, almost black appearance, which fades to a worn brown after a few days exposure to the sun. It has a restless dancing flight as it moves from flower to flower, preferring damp hedgerows and glades, where it may fly in dull weather. Colonies also exist however, on downland, where shrubs such as wild privet, sometimes swarm with Ringlets.

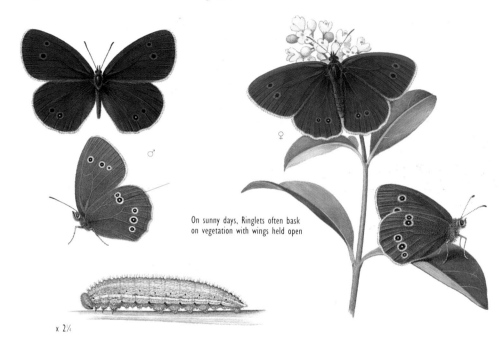

♂

♀

On sunny days, Ringlets often bask on vegetation with wings held open

x 2¼

**KEY FEATURES:** Upperside of male very dark with faint eye-spots, the female is paler with eye-spots clearer, particularly on the underside. There is no spot in space 4, which separates the twin spots near the costa from the other three. The white continuous wing-fringes are conspicuous against darker vegetation. Occasionally specimens occur with the eye-spots on the underside elongated or absent altogether.

**HABITAT:** Found mainly in damp wooded glades and overgrown hedgerows as well as amongst bushes and scrub on downland.

**FREQUENCY:** Widespread and often very common throughout most of central Europe as far north as central Fennoscandia.

**LIFE HISTORY:** The eggs are dropped amongst mixed grasses, with many species recorded as larval foodplants; these include, tor grass, timothy, cock's foot and tufted hair-grass. The sluggish caterpillar feeds at night, including mild winter evenings, resting at the base of grasses during the daytime. Similar to but rather hairier than the brown form of the Gatekeeper caterpillar, it lives for about ten months, and pupates in June, on the ground, in a loose silken cocoon. The chrysalis lasts for two weeks and the first butterflies emerge in late June.

| | | | |
|---|---|---|---|
| J | ✓ | | |
| F | ✓ | | |
| M | ✓ | | |
| A | ✓ | | |
| M | ✓ | | |
| J | ✓ | ✦ | 🦋 |
| J | • | ✓ ✦ | 🦋 |
| A | • | ✓ | 🦋 |
| S | ✓ | | |
| O | ✓ | | |
| N | ✓ | | |
| D | ✓ | | |

**Meadow Brown** *Maniola jurtina*

When freshly emerged, the male Meadow Brown is deep brown but the eye-spots on the forewings are ringed with orange, often with a tawny flush below. The underside of the forewing is diagnostic, with a large expanse of orange, which is noticeable in flight. Both species often fly together. (See p.130)

**False Ringlet** *Coenonympha oedippus*

Smaller than the Ringlet, with faint spots on the upperside, more prominent on the hindwings. When present, post-discal spots on the underside of the forewings, are boldest in spaces 2 and 3. On the hindwings, there are 4 or 5 eye-spots in a row, plus a large one, off-set near the costa. The underside has a metallic blue, submarginal band. Rare and declining, found in widely separated regions throughout central Europe, including northern France. It flies from June until August in damp lowland scrub.

**Woodland Brown** *Lopinga achine*

The spots on the grey-brown uppersides lack white pupils, and are boldly ringed yellow. They are repeated on the underside, which is brighter, with buff markings on the forewings and a white internal band on the hindwings. In flight it appears light, greyish-brown and resembles a large, slow flying Speckled Wood. It flies in grassy clearings in mixed woodland, throughout central Europe as far north as southern Sweden and Finland but not Britain. The flight period is June and July.

# Large Heath

*Coenonympha tullia*

Found only on acidic bogs and heaths, mainly in eastern and northern Europe, the Large Heath is a variable butterfly, ranging from pale sandy buff with no spots, to tawny brown, with up to six bold eye-spots on the underside of the hindwings. Like all species of *Coenonympha*, it always settles with its wings closed, so the upperside is rarely seen other than in butterfly collections. Its flight is weak and individuals seldom fly far, spending most of their time, when not feeding or courting, at rest, concealed on the ground or amongst vegetation.

C. *tullia rothliebii*

Cross-leaved heath is a favourite nectar souce for the Large Heath

**KEY FEATURES:** The underside of the forewings usually has one or two eye-spots and a clearly defined pale post-discal streak. The hindwings are dark at the base and lighten gradually towards the margins. They range from being heavily spotted, to unmarked but the light post-discal marking is consistently bold from the costa to vein 4 and reappears weakly in space 1.

**HABITAT:** Wet, peaty marshes and heaths, with scattered trees, up to 800m.

**FREQUENCY:** Declining in some places through drainage and exploitation of peatland habitats but, in good years, healthy colonies may produce thousands of butterflies.

**LIFE HISTORY:** The comparatively large egg is laid in tussocks of cotton grass or on various species of sedge. It hatches after two weeks and the green and yellow striped caterpillar feeds by day, remaining otherwise, concealed deep in grassy tussocks. It hibernates when less than 1cm in length and some individuals continue to feed through the following year and hibernate for a second time. The chrysalis is suspended deep in the vegetation and lives for about three weeks before hatching. Butterflies are on the wing from mid-June until August in a single brood.

All *Coenonympha* settle with wings closed, so emphasis is given to descriptions of the undersides.

C. t. *scotica*      C. t. *tiphon*      C. t. *rothliebii*

Range of markings on the underside of the Large Heath

## LOOKALIKES

**Pearly Heath** *Coenonympha arcania*
More brightly marked on the upperside, with wide, dark borders. Undersides of the hindwings have a broad, irregular cream band which tapers towards the anal angle and six eye-spots, boldest in spaces 2, 3 and 6. Found from May until August in southern Scandinavia, central Europe but not Britain.

**Chestnut Heath** *Coenonympha glycerion*
Sexes are distinct, the female is larger, with buff-orange forewings. Underside forewing spot is usually absent, those on the hindwings, small, and more even in size, with pale blotches, prominent only in spaces 1, 4 and 5. Flies from June until August in central and eastern Europe as far north as southern Finland.

**False Ringlet** *Coenonympha oedippus*
The bold eye-spot in space 6 of the hindwing is more isolated and all eye-spots are ringed pale yellow, these are orange in the Scarce Heath. (See p.134)

**Scarce Heath** *Coenonympha hero*
Like a small False Ringlet but with any eye-spots on the upperside ringed dusky orange. Underside of forewings with small eye-spot, hindwings with six bold eye-spots ringed with orange, which continues to the margin and contains a silvery-blue line. Rare in parts of France and Germany, eastwards, including southern Fennoscandia, from May until July.

# Small Heath

*Coenonympha pamphilus*

The weak, low flight of this common little ochreous butterfly, easily identifies it in Britain, with only the local Large Heath at all similar. In southern Europe however, a further 12 species of *Coenonympha* occur in varying forms, causing some confusion. It flies in a variety of grassy, flowery habitats, dancing amongst the vegetation on warm days and resting on dead flower heads, when it is dull and at night.

♂

♀

Adult roosting

Small Heath butterflies always feed and rest with their wings closed

x 2¼

**KEY FEATURES:** Similar to the Scottish sub-species of the Large Heath, the Small Heath, has at most, tiny white pupils in place of eye-spots, on the underside of the hindwings. The pale mark across the wing is duller, although the contrast between the discal and post-discal regions is clearer in the Small Heath.

**HABITAT:** Grassy places from sea level to mountain slopes.

**FREQUENCY:** Very common throughout, except the very north west of Fennoscandia.

**LIFE HISTORY:** Eggs are laid singly on fescues and meadow grass and hatch after two weeks. Caterpillars feeds mainly at night and hibernate at varying stages in their growth. Feeding continues in the spring and by late April the largest caterpillars pupate, low down in the grasses. The first butterflies appear in May and in some localities three broods may fly, lasting into October.

# Speckled Wood

*Pararge aegeria*

**M**ost often seen basking with wings half open on vegetation, in sun dappled woodland glades, the male Speckled Wood is fiercely territorial and attacks rival males who wander into his domain. One of the first butterflies to emerge in the spring, unlike most, it is not a lover of open sunny places, nor an avid seeker of flowers, preferring to feed on honey-dew produced by aphids.

2nd brood ♂

Male 2nd brood Speckled Wood basking on bramble leaves

P. aegeria aegeria

| J | ✱ ✱ |   |
|---|-----|---|
| F | ✱ ✱ |   |
| M | ✱ ✱ | ✸ |
| A | · ✱ | ✸ |
| M | · ✱ ✱ | ✸ |
| J | · ✱ ✱ | ✸ |
| J | · ✱ ✱ | ✸ |
| A | · ✱ ✱ | ✸ |
| S | · ✱ ✱ | ✸ |
| O | · ✱ ✱ | ✸ |
| N | ✱ ✱ |   |
| D | ✱ ✱ |   |

**KEY FEATURES:** The male has a sex-brand beneath the cell of the forewing. In northern Europe sub-species *tircis* with cream coloured spots is predominant but further south specimens becomemore orange, sub-species *aegeria*. The hindwings have a scalloped margin and a row of three or four white pupiled spots.

**HABITAT:** Leafy woodland glades and lanes where the sunlight is broken.

**FREQUENCY:** Common and widely distributed throughout Europe.

**LIFE HISTORY:** The egg is laid on a wide range of grasses, growing in warm sheltered places, including, meadow grass, wood false brome, cock's foot and Yorkshire fog. The caterpillar of the late summer brood is unusual, in that it either hibernates, or pupates and spends the winter as a chrysalis. These hatch as early as March but the hibernating caterpillars produce butterflies later in the spring. In warm summers three broods may appear with old, worn specimens still flying in mid October.

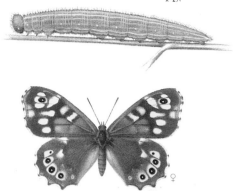

x 2¼

Butterflies of the first brood have larger cream spots than later broods. Caterpillars take from one to six months to reach full size.

## LOOKALIKES

**Woodland Brown** *Lopinga achine*
Sometimes flies in company with the Speckled Wood but is larger and slower in flight. It also basks with wings half open, when it is possible to see the rows of large blind spots, which are repeated on the underside. Flies only in June and July, in central France and Germany eastwards to southern Finland and Sweden. (See p.134)

**Wall** *Lasiommata megera*
Fond of settling on paths and walls, in a similar pose to the Speckled Wood. However, the Wall is more likely to be confused further south, where the ground colour of the Speckled Wood is more orange. It prefers sunnier, open places and its flight is quicker, interspersed with glides. (See p.140)

**Ringlet** *Aphantopus hyperantus*
Another dark woodland butterfly fond of basking in the sun. The upperside only has faint eye-spots, which, on the underside form clear, isolated 'ringlets'. Flies from late June until mid-August. (See p.131)

# Wall

*Lasiommata megera*

The Wall is a widespread and generally common European butterfly but in Britain, its populations have fluctuated throughout the century and in the past decade or so, it has been quite scarce. It spends much of its time basking with wings half open on sun-baked ground, then dancing jerkily along and settling after a few moments. An alert butterfly that can be difficult to approach and frustrating to photograph, further south it often falls prey to lizards.

The Wall spends much of its time concealed or basking on the ground

| | |
|---|---|
| J | ∕ |
| F | ∕ |
| M | ∕ |
| A | ∕ ∕ ✷ |
| M | · ∕ ✷ |
| J | · ∕ ✷ |
| J | · ∕ ∕ ✷ |
| A | · ∕ ∕ ✷ |
| S | · ∕ ✷ |
| O | · ∕ ∕ ✷ |
| N | ∕ |
| D | ∕ |

**KEY FEATURES:** When basking the bold black eye-spots and bright yellow-orange ground colour, are distinctive. The male has a broad sex-brand crossing the forewings, the undersides of the sexes are similar.

**HABITAT:** Sunny paths, field edges, downland slopes and disused railway lines.

**FREQUENCY:** Generally common but populations vary and colonies rarely contain very large numbers.

**LIFE HISTORY:** The egg is laid singly, in warm sheltered places, on grasses such as cock's foot, tor grass and wavy hair-grass. It hatches after 10 days and the caterpillars of the summer brood over-winter, feeding occasionally when it is mild. The chrysalis varies in colour, from yellowish-green to almost black; it is suspended amongst grass stems and butterflies emerge after two weeks. Three broods are produced in warm summers, lasting from April until October.

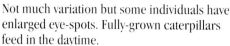

## LOOKALIKES

Not much variation but some individuals have enlarged eye-spots. Fully-grown caterpillars feed in the daytime.

♂ f. *borealis* Fennoscandia

**Large Wall** *Lasiommata maera*
Distributed further to the north east of Europe than the Wall but absent from Britain. Its flight is similar but it is larger with less extensive orange markings. This is most noticeable in Fennoscandia where, in the male, only the eye-spots are ringed with orange, giving an overall dark appearance. It flies in dry, rocky terrain from May until September and is single brooded in the north, with two broods further south.

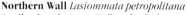

**Northern Wall** *Lasiommata petropolitana*
Smaller than the Large Wall, with which it sometimes flies, the Northern Wall is found along woodland rides and stony paths and often rests on tree trunks. The cell of the forewings has 2 or 3 dark bars and the hindwings have a distinct dark line at the edge of the discal area. Occurs in Fennoscandia and southern Germany southwards. The flight period is from April until August.

**Speckled Wood** *Pararge aegeria*
The southern sub-species *aegeria* is like the Wall, slightly redder orange and with wavy margins to the wings. However it flies in half-shaded, dappled sunlight and avoids sunny, dry, open places. (See p.138)

# Grizzled Skipper

*Pyrgus malvae*

One of eight species of *Pyrgus* Skipper to be found in the region, the Grizzled Skipper is the most widespread, and the only one to occur in Britain. All are rapid fliers that dart busily about in the sunshine but in dull weather and at night they rest, often communally, on grass or flower heads. Although yellow or white flowers are sometimes visited, males spend most of their time basking on the ground, ready to attack trespassing males, or pursue possible mates.

Male Grizzled Skippers basking on the leaves of wild strawberry, one of the larval foodplants

Small groups of Grizzled Skippers may sometimes be found roosting together on dead flowerheads

| | |
|---|---|
| J | ♪ |
| F | ♪ |
| M | ♪ |
| A | ♪ ♥ |
| M · | ♪ ♥ |
| J · | ✦ ♥ |
| J · | ✦ ♪ ♥ |
| A · | ✦ ♪ ♥ |
| S | ♪ |
| O | ♪ |
| N | ♪ |
| D | ♪ |

**KEY FEATURES:** The smallest and most distinctly chequered of all the *Pyrgus* Skippers, with the white hindwing markings, as clear as those of the forewings. The male, which has a fold of scent-scales along the costa of the forewings, is hairier than the female, which may be slightly larger, with a blacker ground colour.

**HABITAT:** Uncultivated flowery slopes, sunny woodland clearings and disused railway lines.

**FREQUENCY:** The commonest Skipper of the group, widespread but absent from northern Britain and northern Fennoscandia.

**LIFE HISTORY:** The egg is laid singly on the upperside of leaves of various members of the Rose family, including, wild strawberry, cinquefoil, agrimony and bramble. The small caterpillar emerges after about ten days and constructs a silken shelter from which it feeds. As it grows, it forms a tent of rolled leaves, the larval stage lasting for two months. Pupation takes place at the base of the foodplant in a silken cocoon. One brood is produced in the north, with occasionally a second in hot summers, and in the south.

Occasionally specimens with expanded white markings may occur. The caterpillar is slow growing and sluggish spending most of its time concealed in its tubular retreat.

## LOOKALIKES

The following group of 7 *Pyrgus* Skippers are similar. However, they often bask in the sunshine with wings outspread, giving the photographer the chance of recording most of the uppersurface. Because there is some individual variation, some species can only be positively identified by examination of their genitalia. The main larval foodplants are *Potentillas* and other members of the Rose family.

**Large Grizzled Skipper** *Pyrgus alveus*
Bigger and browner, with the white markings less bold on the forewings and obscure on the hindwings. The underside of the hindwings is grey-green, strongly marked with white, including the costal margin. Found on flowery slopes, usually above 900m, in central and eastern continental Europe but not Britain. In Scandinavia the smaller sub-species *scandinavicus* flies over stony, sparsely vegetated ground. Flies in a single brood, from June until August.

**Oberthur's Grizzled Skipper** *Pyrgus armoricanus*
Very like the Large Grizzled Skipper but upperside more yellowish-grey with well developed white markings and with the underside ochreous, rather than grey-green. Flies in the lowlands up to 1,300m as far north as southern Sweden, where populations don't overlap. Flies in two broods, from May until August.

x 2¼

**Olive Skipper** *Pyrgus serratulae*
Upperside forewing markings, reduced to small spots, those on the hindwings obscure. The female often has a brassy-olive tinge. The underside of the hindwings is olive-grey with clear white markings. Flies usually in flowery places from lowlands to mountain slopes over 2,000m. Found in central France and Germany southwards.

*P. c. cirsii*

**Carline Skipper** *Pyrgus carlinae*
The sub-species *cirsii* flies locally in central France and southern Germany in July and August. The forewing spots are bold, those on the hindwings prominent, sometimes arrow-shaped on submargins. The underside of the hindwings is dull ochreous-red. Occurs in flowery places rarely up to 1,300m, and sometimes flies with the Olive Skipper.

*143*

## Safflower Skipper *Pyrgus carthami*

Uppersides are well marked, with pale grey hairs around the wing bases. Markings on the hindwings creamy and elongated. The yellow-grey markings on the underside of the hindwings have distinct dark edges. Found in central France and south eastern Germany where it may be quite common in July and August.

## Alpine Grizzled Skipper *Pyrgus andromedae*

Spots on the upperside, reduced on the forewings but usually with one to three discal spots at the base of spaces 1 and 2. On the hindwings the markings are obscure on the upperside and on the underside, in space 1, there is a conspicuous white spot and streak. Flies in the Alps, just into southern Germany and northern Fennoscandia, in June and July.

## Northern Grizzled Skipper *Pyrgus centaureae*

Found in damp flowery places in June and July, only in central and northern Fennoscandia. The white markings are large and well defined, especially on the hindwings, rather like a big Grizzled Skipper. On the underside the markings are strongly contrasting, and the veins, distinctly pale.

## Red Underwing Skipper *Spialia sertorius*

This and other *Spialia* Skippers that occur further south, can be separated from other Skippers by examining the fringes of the forewings, which have feint or no checkering at the end of vein 4. The hindwings are also distinctive, having a cluster of small spots in the centre. The underside of the hindwings are pale brick-red, more ochreous in the first brood, with a large round spot on the costa. Found throughout France, Belgium and Germany, except the extreme north. Flies in diverse flowery habitats from April to June and again in July and August.

# Dingy Skipper
*Erynnis tages*

**D**ull and moth-like, the Dingy Skipper is a sun loving insect which spends much of its life basking on or near the ground. At night and in poor weather, it rests on grass or dead flower heads, in a characteristic pose, with wings folded, roof-like over its back. Its flight is fast and whirring, sometimes causing it to be mistaken for the Grizzled Skipper but it appears browner than its smaller relative. It is one of the first Skippers of the year, appearing at the end of April in good years.

Dingy Skipper on the flowers of bird'sfoot trefoil, the usual larval foodplant

At night the Dingy Skipper rests, moth-like, on the heads of flowers and grasses

Irish form *baynesi* ♀

**KEY FEATURES:** Forewings mottled brown and grey, with three white dots on the costa, near the wing tips, and a row of spots around the margins of the wings. The male has a fold of scent-scales along the costa, (shown unfolded on the right forewing, overleaf) but otherwise the sexes are alike. The underside is not seen as often as other butterflies.

**HABITAT:** Uncultivated downland, woodland clearings, heaths and under-cliffs, where an abundance of bird's foot trefoil grows.

**FREQUENCY:** Becoming less common in north western Europe, otherwise widespread and common but absent from northern Fennoscandia and parts of northern Britain.

**LIFE HISTORY:** The orange egg is laid on bird's foot trefoil and less often on horseshoe vetch. The small caterpillar constructs a shelter of leaves in which it feeds, these are enlarged as it grows, and by the autumn, when fully grown, it hibernates within the leafy cocoon. After more than ten months as a caterpillar it pupates and lives as a chrysalis for the next 4 to 5 weeks. Butterflies start to emerge in late April or May in a single brood, though in good years, and in the south, a second brood may appear in July and August.

| | | | | |
|---|---|---|---|---|
| J | | ✦ | | |
| F | | ✦ | | |
| M | | ✦ | | |
| A | | ✦ | ✦ | 🦋 |
| M | • | | ✦ | 🦋 |
| J | • | ✦ | | 🦋 |
| J | • | ✦ | ✦ | 🦋 |
| A | • | ✦ | ✦ | 🦋 |
| S | | ✦ | | |
| O | | ✦ | | |
| N | | ✦ | | |
| D | | ✦ | | |

Fold of scent scales

# LOOKALIKES

x 2¼

**Mallow Skipper** *Carcharodus alceae*
Occurs commonly in Europe, as far north as central Germany and north-western France, where it flies over warm flowery terrain. The colours are more clearly defined on the forewings than the Dingy Skipper and include white opaque spots. Markings on the hindwings are indistinct and the margins are scalloped. Several broods may appear from April until October. The caterpillar feeds mainly on mallow.

**Tufted Marbled Skipper** *Carcharodus flocciferous*
Larger and greyer than the Mallow Skipper with the pale markings better developed, particularly in the centre of the hindwings. The underside of the forewings have a conspicuous tuft of hair, hence the name, and the ground colour of the hindwings is grey-green. Flies from May until August in two broods, and has a more southerly distribution, just reaching into southern Germany and eastern France.

Two day-flying moths are often confused with the Dingy Skipper. Both are similar in flight and in their resting posture but their distinctive patterns and thread-like antennae should help in positive identification. They occur in the same flowery meadows and downland habitats, and the caterpillars of both feed on clovers and other Legumes.

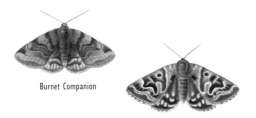
Burnet Companion

Mother Shipton

**Burnet Companion** *Euclidia glyphica*
This common, day-flying moth, occurs in the same habitats as the Dingy Skipper and flies in late June and July, sometimes over-lapping with late flying Skippers. Its general appearance is brown but the hindwings are distinctly orange.

**Mother Shipton** *Callistege mi*
Named after the pattern on the forewings, which resemble the witch-like face of the legendary Mother Shipton. It flies in sunshine, from late May and throughout June in the same grassy places as the Dingy Skipper. Once disturbed it is difficult to approach and must be carefully stalked by the photographer.

# Chequered Skipper

*Carterocephalus palaemon*

Extinct in England for over 20 years, this attractive, lively little butterfly, was only discovered in western Scotland less than 60 years ago, where it still exists in healthy isolation. Here and in other parts of Europe, it flies in damp, woodland clearings, where it feeds avidly from the flowers of bugle, bluebell and thistles. Its flight is typically Skipper-like, fast and difficult to follow, with periods spent basking with wings half open on vegetation.

Female Chequered Skipper at rest

♂

Woodland flowers like bluebells and bugle are visited by the Chequered Skipper in springtime

**KEY FEATURES:** The yellow and black chequering is distinctive when the butterfly is closely observed but confusion can arise when it is in flight. Sexes are alike, although the female may be slightly larger.

**HABITAT:** Damp, well vegetated woodland margins and clearings with an abundance of wild flowers.

**FREQUENCY:** Local, though sometimes fairly common, more frequent further south.

**LIFE HISTORY:** The egg is laid on various species of grass, including, wood false brome, tor and purple moor grass, it hatches after ten days. The small caterpillar soon constructs a tubular retreat of grass blades in which to shelter, these are enlarged as it grows. After three months, and fully grown, it becomes buff coloured and prepares for hibernation amongst dead grasses. In the spring it constructs another more substantial shelter, and without feeding, pupates in April. The single brood is on the wing in May and June.

| | | |
|---|---|---|
| J | / | |
| F | / | |
| M | / | |
| A | / ▸ | |
| M | • ▸ | 🦋 |
| J | • / | 🦋 |
| J | • / | |
| A | / | |
| S | / | |
| O | / | |
| N | / | |
| D | / | |

The size of the yellow spots is variable, and those on the hindwings are paler than the forewings. The caterpillar changes from pale blue-green to buff in the autumn.

x 2⅓

## Lookalikes

**Duke of Burgundy** *Hamearis lucina*
Superficially like the Chequered Skipper but the wings are broader, and the undersides of the hindwings have two clear, white bands. Distributions in Britain do not overlap. (See p.76)

**Northern Chequered Skipper**
*Carterocephalus silvicolus*
The upperside of the male is yellower with the dark discal markings reduced to three or four spots and a row of marginal spots on the forewings. The female is similar to the Chequered Skipper but the yellow is confluent and there is an additional yellow spot near the costa, on the hindwings. Found in Fennoscandia and northern Germany, where it flies in marshy woodland clearings in May and June.

**Large Chequered Skipper** *Heteropterus morpheus*
The dark upperside and low bobbing flight is distinctive. Females have more white spots on the forewings, but the underside of the sexes are alike, similar to a large, bold, Chequered Skipper. Found locally in Jersey, western and northern France, Belgium, Germany and occasionally southern Scandinavia. It flies in June and July, in damp forest clearings and woodland margins with plenty of flowers. The caterpillar feeds on various grasses and reeds.

# Small Skipper
*Thymelicus sylvestris*

The restless, buzzing flight of this little golden butterfly, is typical of the family but confusion can arise, as it shares it grassy habitats with several other similar species, which dart about in the sunshine. Between bouts of feeding, when it favours knapweeds, thistles and other purple flowers, it basks on vegetation, with forewings swept back at an angle and hindwings held flat.

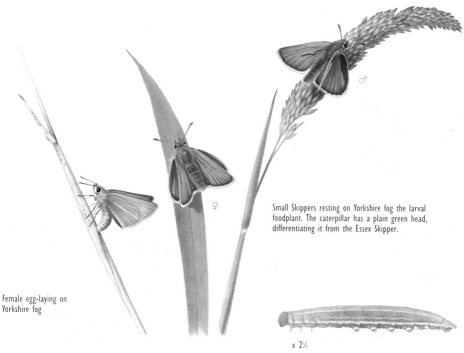

♂

♀

Small Skippers resting on Yorkshire fog the larval foodplant. The caterpillar has a plain green head, differentiating it from the Essex Skipper.

Female egg-laying on Yorkshire fog

x 2¼

**KEY FEATURES:** The sex-brand of the male is long, curved and conspicuous. The sexes are similar on the undersides, with the tips of the forewings and the upper two-thirds of the hindwings greenish-grey, and the rest light fulvous. The underside of the antennae is orange.

**HABITAT:** Rough, grassy downland, flowery roadside verges and woodland clearings.

**FREQUENCY:** Common and widely distributed throughout Europe, as far north as Denmark and northern England.

**LIFE HISTORY:** The eggs are laid in rows, tucked into the sheaths of grasses, mainly Yorkshire fog or creeping soft-grass. The tiny caterpillars hatch after three weeks and immediately spin little cocoons in which to hibernate. They emerge in the spring and feed on grass blades, each constructing a tubular shelter. Full grown in May, pupation takes place in a shelter of grass blades. Butterflies emerge after a further three weeks, in a single brood, from mid-June until early August, although further south they may appear earlier.

The upperside of both sexes is clear fulvous orange ,with the underside of the tips of the antennae also orange.

## LOOKALIKES

Undersides of the anntenae of the Small and Essex Skippers

**Large Skipper** *Ochlodes venatus*
A common but larger species, with a brighter, more variegated upperside. It usually appears on the wing a couple of weeks earlier than the Small Skipper but often feeds with it on the same flower heads. (See p.151)

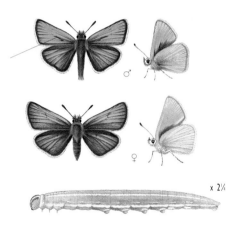

x 2¼

x 2¼

**Essex Skipper** *Thymelicus lineola*
Very similar to the Small Skipper but differs in the following respects. The sex-brands of the male are short, straight and inconspicuous, and the veins near the margin of the wings are suffused darker, especially in the female. The underside is straw coloured with less contrast. The best means of identification, are the tips of the antennae, which appear as though dipped in black paint. With a similar distribution but includes southern Fennoscandia and only as far north as the Midlands in England. Over-winters in the egg stage, the caterpillar differs in having a brown and white striped head. Flight period from May until August, in one generation.

**Lulworth Skipper** *Thymelicus acteon*
Restricted in England to south Dorset, otherwise found throughout Europe, as far north as northern Germany but absent from Holland and Fennoscandia. Rather darker than its two small relatives, usually with a bright, crescent-shaped band on the forewings, more prominent in the female. The underside is unicolorous greenish-orange, with a faint paler band on the forewings of the female. The life-cycle is like that of the Small Skipper, though the eggs are laid on tor grass. In the south it flies from May until August but in Britain, does not appear until mid-July.

# Large Skipper

*Ochlodes venatus*

**T**he commonest, most conspicuous and robust of all the 'orange' Skippers, the male Large Skipper spends much of its time perching alertly on vegetation, ready to dart out at passing insects. Other males are vigorously attacked but females who enter his territory are courted with enthusiasm. A sun loving insect with a preference for purple flowers such as thistles and knapweeds, it is a regular garden visitor and will sup nectar from a variety of garden flowers with its long tongue.

Males perch alertly ready to defend their territory

♂

♀

Male and female Large Skippers perching on cock's foot, the favoured larval foodplant

**KEY FEATURES:** The upperside is rich fulvous, with darker borders, and a prominent black sex-brand on the forewings of the male. The underside is paler, green and orange, with a row of yellow post-discal spots, sometimes very faint.

**HABITAT:** Rough grassy places in diverse habitats, including, flowery meadows, road-side verges, woodland rides, coastal cliffs and dunes.

**FREQUENCY:** Common throughout most of Europe, as far north as southern Scotland and central Fennoscandia.

**LIFE HISTORY:** The egg is laid singly on grass blades of cock's foot, wood false brome and purple moor grass, among others. The caterpillar hatches after two to three weeks and immediately constructs a tubular retreat in which to live. When it is about half an inch long, in September, it prepares for hibernation. It re-emerges in March and continues to feed until May, when it pupates deep in a grassy tussock. The butterfly is single brooded and flies from June until August.

| | | |
|---|---|---|
| J | / | |
| F | / | |
| M | / | |
| A | / | |
| M | / ) | |
| J | · | 🦋 |
| J | · / | 🦋 |
| A | · / | 🦋 |
| S | / | |
| O | / | |
| N | / | |
| D | / | |

x 1½

## LOOKALIKES

Little variation occurs in the Large Skipper. The caterpillar lives, concealed in a tubular retreat, amongst grass blades.

x 1½

**Silver-spotted Skipper** *Hesperia comma*
Like the Large Skipper but the uppersides have more clearly defined yellow spots, particularly the female. The male's sex-brand, has a light central stripe. The underside is olive-green, with prominent silvery white spots. The egg over-winters, and the caterpillar, which feeds mainly on sheep's fescue, is dark olive-grey. The butterfly lives on open flowery slopes, it is widespread and fairly common throughout Europe but in Britain is restricted to warm, south facing downland slopes in southern England. Its flight is more urgent than any of its close relatives, and it avidly seeks nectar in the summer sunshine of July and August.

**Small Skipper** *Thymelicus sylvestris* and
**Essex Skipper** *T. lineola*
Both the two common, small 'orange' Skippers could be confused with the Large Skipper, but their more delicate build and plain wings are diagnostic. (See p.149)

# Butterfly Conservation

Everyone, regardless of their expertise, can make a contribution to our knowledge of butterflies, for it is due to the observations of enthusiastic amateurs that much of our present knowledge exists.

A great deal, however, is yet to be learned and new discoveries and information about the natural world, make every venture into the countryside potentially exciting.

Even the simple act of recording of common butterflies in the garden can be useful in assessing yearly fluctuations in numbers, thus building up an overall picture of the fortunes or misfortunes of different species. The more that is known about a butterfly, the better the chances of maintaining the correct habitat requirements, or recreating a habitat to encourage the expansion of populations.

The practice of collecting large numbers of dead specimens, for no other reason than to have a complete set, like the stamp collector, has become less acceptable, and unnecessary in Britain. Nevertheless, we should remember that many lepidopterists, such as F.W. Frohawk and J.C. Dale, from whom we learned so much, collected thousands of butterflies throughout their lifetimes. Many of these collections still exist in museums, and much of our present knowledge is based on the data contained in them. It is also a fact that many people, myself included, who have grown to love and admire butterflies and moths, and the countryside where they live, started their interests as small children, with a basic collection of common butterflies. With all the resources available today, however, young butterfly enthusiasts have very little need to begin their own collections. Further into southern Europe, where there is a far greater diversity of very similar butterflies, it may be necessary to preserve a greater number of specimens for positive identification, in order to establish the correct information.

In certain habitats, some butterflies are regarded as key indicator species, suggesting that if they occur in reasonable numbers, the habitat is in healthy condition and probably contains plants and other animals that thrive only where there has been no interference with fertilisers, herbicides, pesticides and other agricultural practices. Sadly, in recent decades, no one can have failed to notice the decline of butterflies in northern Europe. In Britain alone, nearly half our butterflies are declining, and are regarded as being in danger of extinction. Organisations like Butterfly Conservation, with around 10,000 members, do excellent work throughout Britain in publicising and helping the plight of butterflies, but no amount of voluntary work alone will reverse the decline. There needs to be greater control over land development, road building, water management, farming methods, pollution, and general use and misuse of the countryside. Since the Wildlife and Countryside Act 1981, important sites supporting some of our most endangered butterflies, have continued to be damaged or destroyed, despite the protection of SSSI (Site of Special Scientific Interest) designation. Most recently, for example, the construction of just one bypass has damaged three SSSI. As well as controlling access to designated sites, the activities of road builders, developers and water authorities should also be held in check.

We can all help by joining conservation organisations, and by lobbying our local MPs and other political organisations. Changes in the law are needed to protect our countryside and the wildlife it supports.

# Glossary

**Abdomen** The end section of a butterfly's body comprising of ten segments (see diagram p.9)

**Aberration** A butterfly with abnormal markings, much sought after by collectors

**Anal Angle** The lower outside angle of the fore- and hindwings (see diagram p.9)

**Adroconia** Specialised scent scales grouped in clusters on the wings of some male butterflies, often forming conspicuous bands

**Antenna/Antennae** (plural) Paired sensory organs with clubbed tips, attached to the head of a butterfly (see diagram p.9)

**Apex** The outer tip of the wings (see diagram p.9)

**Basal Area** The area of the wing nearest the body (see diagram p.9)

**Caterpillar** The second and growing stage in the life-cycle of a butterfly. See also larva

**Calcareous** Alkaline soil or rock found on chalk and limestone downland

**Cell** An enclosed space running from the base of the fore- and hindwings (see diagram page 9)

**Chrysalis** The third stage in a butterfly's life-cycle prior to its emergence. Also known as a pupa

**Cocoon** A protective silken enclosure, constructed by the caterpillar, prior to its change into a chrysalis

**Coppicing** A method of woodland management involving the periodic harvesting of trees, thus opening up woodland and producing flowery habitats much loved by butterflies

**Costa** The front edge of the fore- and hindwings (see diagram p.9)

**Costal Fold** A fold along the front edge of the forewings of some male butterflies, which contain scent or androconial scales

**Cryptic** Markings which camouflage when a butterfly or moth is at rest

**Discal Area** The central part of the wings (see diagram p.9)

**Femur** The largest of a butterfly's leg joints (see diagram p.9)

**Frenulum** The wing locking mechanism found on the underside of most moths' wings (see diagram p.9)

**Genitalia** Sexual organs found at the tip of the abdomen of butterflies and moths, often used to differentiate similar species

**Girdle** A silken band that supports the chrysalis of certain butterfly species

**Hemimetabolous** Insects belonging to the more primitive orders, such as the dragonflies and cockroaches, which have a less distinct metamorphosis and which lack a pupal stage

**Heterocera** The out-dated name for moths when they were regarded as in a distinct sub-order from the butterflies

**Hibernaculum** A shelter constructed by a hibernating caterpillar

**Holometabolous** Insects, including butterflies and moths, which have a complete metamorphosis with a pupal stage

**Imago** The final, adult stage of an insect's development

**Instar** A stage of growth between a caterpillars skin changes

**Larva/Larvae** (Plural) The second and growing stage in the life-cycle of a butterfly. See also caterpillar

**Lepidoptera** The order of insects to which butterflies and moths belong. Meaning 'scale-winged'

**Metamorphosis** The life-cycle of a butterfly as it changes from egg, to caterpillar, to chrysalis and finally to adult

**Micropyle** A central dimple on a butterfly's egg, sometimes visible with the naked eye, which allows sperm to enter and the developing caterpillar to breath

**Migrant** A butterfly which moves seasonally from one place to another to take advantage of better feeding or breeding sites

**Mimic** To resemble the surrounding vegetation or distasteful organisms, in order to gain protection

**Osmeterium** An unpleasant smelling, forked organ, which can be inflated behind the head of Swallowtail and Apollo caterpillars, to help avoid attack from predators

**Ovipositor** An specialised egg laying organ at the end of some female insects' abdomens

**Ovum/Ova** (Plural) Egg

**Palp/Palpi** (Plural) A pair of sensory organs at the front of the head, either side of the coiled proboscis

**Post Discal Area** An area of the wings (See diagram p.9)

**Proboscis** The tubular tongue of a butterfly held coiled between the palpi when not in use

**Pupa /Pupae** (Plural) The third stage in the life-cycle of a butterfly. Chrysalis

**Rhopalocera** The out-dated name for butterflies, when they were regarded as distinct from moths

**Sex-brand** A cluster of androconial scales, which often form bold markings on the wings of some male butterflies

**Space** An area on the wings of a butterfly between the veins, numbered from 1–12 to help aid identification (see diagram p.9)

**Species** The classification of a group of individuals, with common characteristics, which allow them to breed and reproduce similar, viable offspring

**Sphragis** A hard structure, formed at the end of some female butterflies' abdomens whilst mating, which prevents further matings from other males

**Submarginal area** An area of the wing (see diagram p.9)

**Sub-species** The classification of a group of individuals, which, due to geographic separation, have characteristics that vary from others of the same species

**Tarsus** The end part of the leg, usually containing five segments (see diagram p.9)

**Thorax** The central part of a butterfly's body where the legs and wings are attached (see diagram p.9)

**Tibia** A part of the leg (see diagram p.9)

**Vein** Hardened tubular structure which carries blood and supports the wings in flight

**Venation** The arrangement of veins on a butterfly's wings, often used in separating species and identifying specific areas of the wing (see diagram p.9)

# Further Reading

Please note some of these titles may be out of print but are included because they have been influential in this field of study.

## BRITAIN AND IRELAND

Brooks, M., & Knight, C., (1982) *A Complete Guide to British Butterflies*. Jonathan Cape

Dennis, R.L.H., (1977) *The British Butterflies: Their Origin and Establishment*. E.W. Classey

Emmet, A.M., & Heath, J., (eds). (1989) *The Moths and Butterflies of Great Britain and Ireland Volume 7 pt.1: The Butterflies*. Harley Books

Feltwell, J., (1986) *The Natural History of Butterflies*. Croom Helm

Ford, E.B., (1945) *Butterflies*. Collins

Heath, J., Pollard, E., & Thomas, J.A., (1984) *Atlas of Butterflies in Britain and Ireland*. Viking

Oates, M., (1985) *Garden Plants for Butterflies*. Masterton

Thomas, J.A., (1989) *Hamlyn Guide to the Butterflies of the British Isles*. Hamlyn

Thomas, J.A., & Lewington, R., (1991) *The Butterflies of Britain and Ireland*. Dorling Kindersley

Thomson, G., (1980) *The Butterflies of Scotland*. Croom Helm

South, R., (1906) *The Butterflies of the British Isles*. Fredrick Warne

Frohawk, F.W., (1924) *The Natural History of British Butterflies*. Hutchinson

Frohawk, F.W., (1934) *The Complete Book of British Butterflies*. Ward Lock

## EUROPE

Chinery, M., (1998) *Butterflies of Britain and Europe*. HarperCollinsPublishers

Dal, B., (1982) *The Butterflies of Northern Europe*. Croom Helm

Henriksen, H.J., & Kreutzer, I.B., (1982) *The Butterflies of Scandinavia in Nature*. Skandinavisk Bogforlag, Odense

Tolman, T., & Lewington, R., (1997) *Collins Field Guide Butterflies of Britain and Europe*. HarperCollinsPublishers

Whalley, P., (1980) *Butterfly Watching*. Severn House

Whalley, P., (1981) *The Mitchell Beazley Pocket Guide to Butterflies*. Mitchell Beazley

# Useful Addresses

**Amateur Entomologists' Society**
P.O. Box 8774,
London SW7 5ZG

**British Entomological and Natural History Society**
74 South Audley Street,
London W1Y 5FF

**Butterfly Conservation**
P.O. Box 222, Dedham,
Colchester
Essex CO7 6EY

**Entomological Livestock Group**
11 Rock Gardens,
Aldershot
Hampshire GU11 3AD

**Royal Entomological Society of London**
41 Queen's Gate,
London SW7 5HR

# Index

Admiral, Indian Red 90
Admiral, Poplar 81, 83, **84-5**
Admiral, Red 7, 13, 14, 20, 89, **90-1**, 95
Admiral, Southern White 83, 85
Admiral, White 7, 11, **82-3**, 85, 97
*Aglais urticae* 87, 89, 91, **94-5**
*Agriades glandon* 69
*A. glandon* ssp. *aquilo* 69
*Agrodiaetus amanda* 73
*Agrodiaetus damon* 71
*Agrodiaetus thersites* 75
*Albulina orbitulus* 69
*Amphipyra pyramidea* 8
*Anthocharis cardamines* 33, 35, **38-9**
*Apanteles* sp. 28, 116
*Apanteles glomeratus* 10, 13, 30
*Apatura ilia* 81
*Apatura iris* **80-1**, 83, 85
*Aphantopus hyperantus* 131, **133**, 139
Apollo 16, **26-7**
Apollo, Clouded 27, 29
*Aporia crataegi* **28-9**
*Araschnia levana* 77, 83, **96-7**
*Arethusana arethusa* 122
Argus, Brown 18, 58, **66-7**, 75
Argus, Geranium 67
Argus, Northern Brown 66-7
Argus, Scotch 21, **124-5**
Argus, Silvery 67
*Argynnis adippe* 101, **102-3**
*Argynnis aglaja* **100-1**, 103
*Argynnis laodice* 101
*Argynnis niobe* 103
*Argynnis pandora* 99
*Argynnis paphia* **98-9**
*A. paphia* f. *valezina* 98
*Aricia agestis* **66-7**, 75
*Aricia atraxerxes* 67
*A. atraxerxes* ssp *allous* 67
*Artogeia napi* 33, 39
*Artogeia rapae* 31, **32-3**, 35, 39

Blue, Adonis 18, 23, 71, **72-3**, 75
Blue, Alcon 63
Blue, Alpine 69
Blue, Amanda's 73
Blue, Baton 65
Blue, Chalkhill **70-1**, 73, 75
Blue, Chapman's 75
Blue, Chequered 65
Blue, Common 57, 61, 67, 70-1, 73, **74-5**
Blue, Cranberry 69
Blue, Damon 71
Blue, Dusky Large 63
Blue, Eastern Baton 65
Blue, life cycle 10, 14
Blue, Glandon 69

Blue, Green-underside 61
Blue, Holly 23, 59, **60-1**
Blue, Idas 64-5
Blue, Lang's Short-tailed 57
Blue, Large 13, 18, **62-3**
Blue, Long-tailed **56-7**
Blue, Mazarine 59, 61, **68-9**
Blue, Meleager's 71
Blue, Mountain Alcon 63
Blue, Osiris 59, 69
Blue, Reverdin's 64-5
Blue, Scarce Large 63
Blue, Short-tailed 57, 59, 61
Blue, Silver-studded 10, **64-5**, 67, 75
Blue, Small 12, **58-9**, 61
Blue, Turquoise 73
*Boloria aquilonaris* 109
*Boloria napaea* 109
*Boloria pales* 109
*Brenthis daphne* **105**
*Brenthis ino* **105**
Brimstone 11, 17, 31, 42, **44-5**
Brown, Arran 125
Brown, Dusky Meadow 131
Brown, life cycle 14
Brown, Meadow 14, 21, **130-1**, 134
Brown, Woodland 134, 139
Burnet Companion 8, 146
Butterfly, antennae 7
Butterfly, caterpillar 12-13
Butterfly, definition 6-7
Butterfly, egg 10-11
Butterfly, life-cycle 10-15
Butterfly, structure 9

*Callimorpha dominula* 91
*Callistege mi* 146
*Callophrys rubi* 49
Camberwell Beauty 14, 86, 89
*Carcharodus alceae* 146
*Carcharodus flocciferous* 146
Cardinal 99
*Carterocephalus palaemon* 77, **147-8**
*Carterocephalus silvicolus* 148
*Celastrina argiolus* 59, **60-1**
*Chasara briseis* 120
Cleopatra 45
*Clossiana chariclea* 110
*Clossiana dia* 111
*Clossiana euphrosyne* **106-7**, 109
*C. euphrosyne* f. *fingal* 107
*Clossiana freija* 110
*Clossiana frigga* 110
*Clossiana improba* 111
*Clossiana polaris* 110
*Clossiana selene* 77, 97, 107, **108-9**
*C. selene* f. *hela* 109

*Clossiana thore* 111
*C. thore* ssp *borealis* 111
*Clossiana titania* 111
*C. titania* ssp. *cypris* 111
*Coenonympha arcania* 136
*Coenonympha glycerion* 136
*Coenonympha hero* 136
*Coenonympha oedippus* 134, 136
*Coenonympha pamphilus* **137**
*Coenonympha tullia* **135-6**
*C. tullia* ssp *rothliebii* 136
*C. tullia* ssp *scotica* 136
*C. tullia* ssp *tiphon* 136
*Colias alfacariensis* 43
*Colias croceus* **40-1**
*C. croceus* var. *helice* 40-1
*Colias hecla* 41
*Colias hyale* 41, **42-3**, 45
*Colias myrmidone* 41
*Colias nastes* 43
*Colias palaeno* 43
*Colias phicomone* 43
Colour, in scales 6
Comma 20, 89, **93**
Comma, False 87
Copper, Large 18, 52, **54-5**
Copper, Purple-edged 55
Copper, Purple Shot 55
Copper, Scarce 53, 55
Copper, Small 18, **52-3**
Copper, Sooty 53
Copper, Violet 53
Copper Underwing 8
*Cupido minimus* **58-9**, 61
*Cupido osiris* 59, 69
*Cyaniris semiargus* 59, 61, **68-9**

Danaidae family 19
*Danaus plexippus* **78-9**
Dryad 122
Duke of Burgundy 19, **76-7**, 97, 148

Early Thorn 8
Emperor, Lesser Purple 81
Emperor Moth 8
Emperor, Purple 15, 20, **80-1**, 83, 85
*Erebia aethiops* **124-5**
*Erebia disa* 125
*Erebia epiphron* **127**
*Erebia eriphyle* 128
*Erebia euryale* 125
*Erebia gorge* 129
*Erebia ligea* 125
*Erebia manto* 128
*Erebia medusa* 126
*Erebia melampus* 129
*Erebia mnestra* 129